Ask Suze®

. . . About Wills and Trusts

ALSO BY SUZE ORMAN

You've Earned It, Don't Lose It

Suze Orman's Financial Guidebook

The 9 Steps to Financial Freedom

The Courage to Be Rich

The Road to Wealth

The Laws of Money, The Lessons of Life

The Money Book for the Young, Fabulous & Broke

Women & Money

Riverhead Books
a member of
Penguin Group (USA) Inc.
New York
2007

Ask Suze®

...About Wills and Trusts

Suze Orman

This publication is designed to provide accurate and authoritative information in regard to the subject matter covered. It is published with the understanding that the publisher and author are not engaged in rendering legal, accounting, or other professional services. If legal advice or other professional advice, including financial, is required, the services of a competent professional person should be sought.

While the author has made every effort to provide accurate telephone numbers and Internet addresses at the time of publication, neither the publisher nor the author assumes any responsibility for errors, or for changes that occur after publication.

Ask Suze® is a federally registered mark owned by Suze Orman.

People First, Then Money, Then Things™ is a trademark owned by Suze Orman.

Certified Financial Planner® is a federally registered mark owned by the Certified Financial Planner Board of Standards, Inc.

The term Realtor® is a collective membership mark owned by the National Association of Realtors® and refers to a real estate agent who is a member thereof.

RIVERHEAD BOOKS
a member of
Penguin Group (USA) Inc.
375 Hudson Street
New York, NY 10014

Published simultaneously in Canada

ISBN 978-1-59448-966-2

Printed in the United States of America
1 3 5 7 9 10 8 6 4 2

Book design by Deborah Kerner and Claire Vaccaro

FOREVER MORE

If you've ever had someone close to you die, you know there are no words to describe the pain and loss that follow. And the long period of adjustment after a loved one's death is often complicated by issues concerning money. Sometimes the person who has died has failed to plan ahead. Sometimes those left behind do not understand how to go forward financially.

Everyone will leave loved ones behind when he or she dies. If you want to behave lovingly toward those you leave behind, please take the time now to plan so that, in the event of your death, your family and heirs will not become financially unstable at the precise moment they are most emotionally vulnerable. I urge you to discuss your estate with your spouse or partner, with your children, and with anyone else who will be financially affected by your death. Also, if you are married or hold joint assets with someone else, please take time now to learn everything you can about your joint finances, so that if you are the one left behind you will not have to cope with financial confusion on top of your grief.

Thinking about your own death or the death of a family member is no easy assignment. Neither is contemplating serious illness or incapacity. But planning for the future does not have to make you feel morbid; it can, and probably will, provide you a sense of control over your own life. It's freeing to know that you've protected those you care most about in this life.

This chapter addresses questions people commonly have about how to care for themselves and those they love in case of illness, incapacity, or death. Estate planning is actually a fascinating process, for it involves examining your goals, your values, and your financial priorities. If you plan carefully, you and your family can save thousands or even hundreds of thousands of dollars in probate fees, estate taxes, and attorneys' fees as well as the nuisance of going through an unnecessarily complicated and lengthy probate process. In my experience, once you begin to take steps to protect the future of the people you care about, you will have started down the path toward securing your own financial freedom.

WILLS: DEFINING THE TERMS

What is an estate?

The term "estate" can have more than one meaning. Your taxable *estate* is the sum total of all your financial interests, both money and property. Basically, your taxable estate is made up of everything you own at the time of your death, including life insurance, retirement plans, and IRAs, less your outstanding debts. Your *probate* estate includes only those assets covered by your will.

What is a will?

A will is a legal document that designates how you want your money and property (your estate) to be distributed after your death. It also specifies your wishes regarding funeral and burial arrangements, and, if you have children who are minors, it states whom you request the court to appoint as their guardian.

Who is the testator?

If you are a man and you have created a will, you are called the testator of your will. A woman who has created a will used to be called the testatrix; however, in most legal arenas today the term testator is used without regard to gender.

What is a beneficiary?

A beneficiary is a person or organization designated to receive some or all of your assets upon your death. You can name as many beneficiaries as you like.

What is an executor?

An executor is the person you appoint in your will to settle your estate. This person will have the administrative responsibility of paying your bills and taxes (including estate taxes), supervising the process of locating and safekeeping your assets, and making sure that the wishes expressed in your will are carried out. In essence, an executor is in charge of the estate. A personal representative of an estate may be known as an administrator, executor, or fiduciary, depending on the type of document signed or not signed by you.

What is probate?

Probate is a court procedure by which assets pass from a deceased person to the proper beneficiaries. A judge has the authority to validate a will and then order that the assets subject to the will be distributed. A court order signed by the judge transfers ownership to the beneficiaries—without a court order, the beneficiaries cannot take ownership (with some exceptions), even if they are named in the will. We'll discuss the probate process in greater depth later in this chapter.

The Importance of Having a Will

How do I know if I need a will?

If you want to decide who should receive your assets upon your death—even if all you have is a car—you need a will. If you want to name a person who will be responsible for the care of your young child or children, you need a will. If you want to decide who will take care of your taxes, debts, and financial affairs when you die, you need a will.

What happens if I don't have a will?

You *do* have a will, so to speak, whether you know it or not. Even if you haven't personally drawn up a will, the state you live in has something called intestate succession rules. These intestate rules determine exactly who receives any assets held in your name when you die. Usually, your spouse and children receive your property first; if you aren't survived by a spouse or children, your grandchildren might be next in line, followed by your parents, siblings, nieces, nephews, and cousins. If you die without any relatives, or without relatives that anyone can find, your assets will pass to the state.

If you care about the things you have worked hard for in your lifetime and what will become of them, you need a will. In most cases, you also need a living trust.

What if I am estranged from most of my relatives and don't want them to inherit my assets?

All the more reason to have a will! Most people leave the bulk of their estate to their relatives, and most states assume that this is what you would have wanted, too. If you don't want your relatives to inherit your assets, you have to take the time to create a will and name your beneficiaries.

If I have been living with my life partner for 20 years and she dies without a will, do I have any legal right to the assets we share?

It depends. If you and your life partner own any property or accounts in joint tenancy with right of survivorship, you will be entitled to that property or money. But assuming that you don't have property or accounts held in joint tenancy and your partner does not have a will or a trust, the state will not recognize your relationship for the purpose of distributing your life partner's assets. In that case, your partner's blood relatives, or even the state itself, will receive your partner's assets before you do.

Is jointly held property the only type of asset that will not be disposed of by the state if I die without a will?

No. If you have designated a beneficiary on a retirement account, an annuity, an insurance policy, or a pay-on-death account, for example, the beneficiaries who survive you will receive the money in those accounts whether or not you have a will. These assets will not have to go through the probate procedure, either.

I am so deep in credit card debt at this point that I wouldn't have an estate to leave to anyone. Shouldn't I deal with my debt first, before I spend money to draw up a will?

While it is very important that you map out a strategy for

eliminating your debts, planning for the future of the people you love is the most important, most responsible thing you can do—for them *and* for yourself. In my experience, once you do so, you will gain peace of mind that will help clear a way to financial security. Even if you don't have many assets, a will can help your family with the costs of a funeral or burial. (State law may also allow you to specify burial/cremation directions in a separate letter that's drafted and signed. You may want to sign such a letter and keep a copy outside your safe-deposit box, with the original given to your executor.) When your grieving family goes to see a funeral director, they may not know that you didn't want them to pay thousands of dollars for embalming or an open casket ceremony. Similarly, if someone does not have the clear authority to take care of your personal property—your car, your clothes, or your furniture—your landlord (if you are a renter) may be very confused and not know what to do with them. A will enables you to specify how you would like your personal property and your funeral to be handled.

Another thing to bear in mind is that your estate may be worth more than you think, particularly if you have equity in your home or a life insurance policy through your job. The bottom line is that planning ahead is important no matter how much or how little money you have.

My neighbor and her husband have a joint will, which they said saved them some attorneys' fees. Do you think joint wills are a good idea?

I have to say that I don't. A joint will is a single will shared by two people, usually spouses. It typically contains the same provisions for each person—a husband leaves all his property to his wife, say, and vice versa, and after the death of both spouses the property typically goes to the children. The problem is that, in many states, as soon as one of the signatories dies, the joint will goes into probate. This means that the terms of the will are frozen for the surviving spouse. Though right now it may be hard to imagine ever wanting to alter your will, you should always preserve the right to change your mind. If you should remarry years after the death of your partner and want to will your assets to your new spouse rather than your children, you might be prevented from doing so by an old joint will.

Is a joint will the same as a mutual will?

No. A joint will is a single will shared by two people. Mutual wills are, typically, two separate wills that are identical in most ways, each person's will benefiting the other party. If you and your spouse each sign a will that has mirror or identical provisions, specifying that you leave everything to your partner and he or she leaves everything to you, these are considered mutual wills. You are not bound by promises made together, as you are in a joint will, so either of you can change your mutual will at any time.

I have a house in Maine where I spend my summers, but I spend most of the year in Virginia. Do I need a will for both states?

No. A single will is all you need, and you should have it drawn up in the state where you have your domicile (permanent residence). Get legal advice on establishing your domicile and on any special provisions that need to be included for your property in another state. And with all that property, please seriously consider a revocable living trust. (If you have only a will and not a revocable living trust, your beneficiaries may be required to go through two probates—one in Virginia, and an ancillary probate in Maine.)

My neighbor has a videotaped will. Is that a good idea?
Since most states do not recognize videotaped wills as legally binding, what I assume you mean is that your neighbor has a written will but also had someone videotape her talking about its contents. I sometimes recommend this as a precautionary measure to people who are concerned that someone will challenge the terms of their will or trust. Videotaping may not be necessary for you, but if you decide to do it, it should not cost you very much. Most videographers charge by the hour, and an experienced attorney will usually be able to refer you to someone who can provide this service.

THE KEY PLAYERS

EXECUTORS

What do I have to do if I am named an executor?
First, you must locate the will or trust and all the assets owned by the deceased person (bank and retirement accounts, stocks and bonds, insurance policies, real estate holdings, etc.). Once you have found the will, you must submit it to the probate court for authentication, usually with the assistance of an attorney. Once the will has been validated ("proved"), the court will officially appoint you as the executor of the will and give you a set of documents called letters testamentary. Some states call these letters of authority or letters of appointment. These legally empower you to do things in the estate's name, such as take charge of a bank account. (You will not have the authority to act on the estate's behalf without these letters.) You should get multiple copies of the letters testamentary—at least seven.

As executor, you are responsible for protecting the estate, which means, first and foremost, that you cannot give the beneficiaries any of the assets left to them until the probate court has approved the distribution (unless the laws of the state you're in allow some distributions without court approval). In some states, you are required to identify creditors and debts of the estate to the probate court.

You will need to monitor and record all the expenses and income that the estate pays out and receives while it is in probate.

You should obtain at least 15 certified copies of the death certificate. You may need these to transfer title to real estate or investment holdings, or even to a car. You may also need them to settle any life insurance claims or to close bank or brokerage accounts, if necessary.

You must notify all insurance companies, banks, brokerage firms, retirement plans and administrators, the Veterans Administration, or any other institution that had financial dealings with the deceased person. This includes any institution where the deceased person had joint accounts.

You must pay all bills still owed by the deceased out of a special checking account that you will have to establish in the name of the estate.

Sometimes the deceased's individual bank accounts will be changed into your name, as executor on behalf of the state, so that you can access funds to pay bills for the estate. Any accounts, money, or property held as a joint tenancy with right of survivorship (JTWROS) will go directly to the surviving person whose name appears on the title of that asset.

Before you close any bank accounts, make sure that the surviving spouse's (if relevant) financial needs will continue to be met until the estate is settled. You should also double-check with an estate attorney before closing any accounts.

If there is a safe-deposit box, make a complete inventory of its contents.

Look for the past three years of state and federal income tax returns. Besides providing information about the deceased's holdings, they should be held because the deceased can still be audited for three years after death. You will also be responsible for paying any taxes owed by the deceased to the government.

What kinds of bills still have to be paid after death?
Typically, all of them. Until an estate is settled, regular payments, such as mortgage payments and utility bills, need to be paid each month, as do any credit card bills or loans. Also, any expenses that result from the death or the illness preceding it, such as medical bills, funeral expenses, taxes, and executor, court, and probate fees must be paid. All of these obligations will have to be paid before the estate can be finally distributed.

What if there isn't enough cash in the estate to pay all the expenses due?
The executor will have to start selling off (liquidating) assets from the estate, such as a house or car, in order to cover these bills, even if payments cut into specific bequests for the beneficiaries. Some debts (such as attorney fees) are given priority over other debts, so that no other debt can be paid until these priority debts are settled.

Whom should I choose to be my executor?
Your executor should be someone you trust completely. He or she will sign for everything, manage the selling of your assets if you have debts to settle, and exercise control over your estate. As you can imagine, it is crucial that your executor be a responsible person. It is common to name a spouse or life partner as your executor. When you think about whom to choose, think

about whom you would want to be the first one to arrive at your house after your death and become the keeper of the keys thereafter until everything is settled.

Can an executor get paid?

Yes. The fee varies depending on the state you live in. It is often calculated as a small percentage of the total value of your estate, usually between 2 and 5 percent. An executor's fee can easily be higher, particularly if your executor has to do anything out of the ordinary, in which case he or she may charge the estate additional fees.

Your executor has the power to choose not to be paid, and you can request, but not require, that he or she do this. For most people, serving as an executor can be very demanding, as he or she may be asked to perform many tasks. The amount of time it takes to settle an estate depends on factors beyond the executor's control, including how contentious the heirs are!

Why would an executor choose not to be paid?

It may make financial sense to decline to be paid if the executor is also the main beneficiary (which, again, is common if you have a surviving spouse or partner). Executor's fees are subject to income tax, but inherited property generally is not (the exceptions include retirement plans and traditional IRAs). If you find yourself in this situation and the estate is large enough to be subject to federal estate taxes, ask an attorney or an accountant to help you determine which option will afford you the best tax result. (Executor's fees are deductible for the estate on an estate tax or income tax return.)

Who will act as the executor of my estate if I die without a will?

If you die without a will, there will not be an executor.

Instead, the court will appoint an administrator, who will perform most of the same tasks an executor would have performed, in terms of collecting and paying your debts and distributing your property. The laws of your state determine who serves as the administrator; usually a spouse is chosen first. But the person must petition the court to be appointed, so there is no guarantee about who will actually end up serving.

I am the executor of my father's estate and I've learned that funerals and burials are incredibly expensive! How do I know if I'm paying too much?

People often make very poor decisions when they are arranging funerals and burials, and that's understandable—you are tired, upset, stressed out, and probably don't know much about what you are buying. As a general rule, if a funeral home wants you to purchase something that will cost more than $10,000, you should probably go elsewhere or demand another type of service. A simple, dignified service that you can afford can be just as loving as a lavish one.

Your dad may have burial benefits through his life insurance policy, from the Department of Veterans Affairs (if he was in the service), through his job or a union, or from Social Security. Even if these benefits are modest, there's no reason not to use them if he has them.

Many people are concerned about the high cost of dying. If you are among them, I urge you to read Jessica Mitford's informative and surprisingly funny book, *The American Way of Death Revisited.*

Can an executor be sued?

Yes. As an executor, you are liable for any action you take on behalf of the estate, so you can be sued by the beneficiaries if the estate is managed carelessly. You also can be sued by someone you've contracted with on the estate's behalf. Let's say you hire a gardener to take care of the property surrounding the house of the deceased person until you sell the house, but then the estate doesn't have enough money to pay the gardener. If you, as the executor, entered into a contract with the gardener, you could be personally liable for any damages.

My aunt has just died and in her will she named me the executor of her estate. This is very unexpected, and I'm not sure that I can take on the responsibility right now. Do I have to?

No, you always have the right to refuse to serve as an executor. You don't have to give a reason. This raises an important point: People need to make their wishes known to each other while they are still alive. If your aunt had discussed her choice with you beforehand, you could have told her that you had reservations and she could have made other arrangements. It's not a good idea to surprise anyone with this responsibility. It's also a good idea to designate possible alternate executors in your will.

If you refuse the role of executor and no alternate executors are named in the will, state law sets forth a preferred order for appointment among the options of spouse, child, parent, etc., but anyone can request or refuse appointment.

In addition to the financial aspects of planning my estate, is there anything else I should do to assist my executor or my loved ones after I die?

Although written instructions do not take the place of a will and may not be legally binding, it's not a bad idea to write out a list of instructions about the execution of your will and leave it in an accessible place. This list can state where to find your will and trust instruments (if you have them), bank and brokerage accounts, checkbooks, deeds, insurance policies (if you have them), and safe-deposit or post-office boxes. Alternatively, if you don't feel comfortable having all this information in one place, the list might simply mention the names and phone numbers of your attorney, financial adviser, and primary doctor. Finally, the list might contain other practical information, such as any specific wishes you have regarding your funeral and burial or any unusual maintenance needed for your house or your pet. If you do not have a friend or family member who is very knowledgeable about the details of your daily life, instructions such as these can be particularly helpful. There is no need to repeat anything you've already included in your will.

Generally, if most of your property is held in a revocable living trust, and your will has been properly organized and you have left clear instructions behind, you will greatly simplify your executor's job.

Beneficiaries

What happens if my beneficiaries die before I do?

You should designate alternate beneficiaries to receive your assets. In other words, you would state that you want your wife to receive all of your assets, but if she were to predecease you, then your assets should go to your daughter; your daughter becomes the alternate beneficiary to your wife. If the will is properly drafted, your attorney will have asked you to make decisions that cover every possibility.

My will talks about my beneficiaries receiving my residual estate. What does that mean?

A well-written will designates someone to receive your residual estate, which is whatever is left of your assets after beneficiaries have received their specific bequests. If you said, for example, that you wanted your local public library to receive anything left in your residual estate and one of your beneficiaries predeceased you, the portion of your estate that the deceased person would have received will pass to the library (if no alternate is named or called for under your state's law).

Some states will protect certain types of bequests from lapsing in this way. The most common example would be if you left something to your child but your child predeceased you. In some states, that bequest is automatically passed down to your child's children if you have not designated otherwise.

Can I have more than one residual beneficiary?

Sure. You can say that you want all your surviving children to share your residual estate equally (this is very common), or you can name several people and have them divide your residual estate, either equally or according to some other set of percentages specified in your will.

What if my beneficiary is a minor?

States do not usually allow children under the age of 18 to hold property valued at more than $2,500 to $5,000 as individuals. In your will you can designate a guardian to manage the property until your child reaches a certain age, but many states have complicated requirements for regular court supervision of property held for children. If, under a living trust and possibly under a will, you establish a trust and name a trustee to manage your child's property, you can save your child the often substantial costs of dealing with the courts. You will also give the trustee greater flexibility in managing the assets in the trust, as you can set the terms you want for the age(s) at which the children can gain access to the money, and what it can or can't be used for. For example, you can allow the trustee to hold back distributions if the child is going through a difficult time with alcohol or other substance abuse, or a divorce.

If my mother's will said that she wanted to leave everything to me, but she had an old life insurance policy that named her sister as the beneficiary, do I have any right to that life insurance money?
No, you don't. Retirement accounts, insurance policies, and other assets that require or have a beneficiary designation are entirely separate from, and are not controlled by, a will.

What happens if I have made specific monetary bequests in my will and I die without sufficient funds to cover gifts to my beneficiaries?
You can't give what you don't have. If your estate doesn't contain enough money to cover all your bequests, then all your bequests will be proportionally reduced. The system by which the court prioritizes those reductions is called an abatement. If, on the other hand, you have left a specific bequest—say, your car—to your daughter, but in the intervening years, you stopped driving and sold that car, then your daughter would not be entitled to any adjustment to make up for it.

I lived with my partner for ten years before he died, unexpectedly and without a will. I know he wanted me to inherit everything. How do I prove that?
I'm sorry to say that, generally, if your partner did not make provisions for you with a will or a revocable living trust or if you don't have jointly owned property, you have no inheritance rights at all. That is why it is so important that you do not assume things will take care of themselves after you're gone.

What if something terrible happens, like a car accident or a plane crash, and my husband and I die at the same time?

In most cases, the state will assume that each of you predeceased the other, which means that each of your estates will be distributed as if the other person had died first. You can request a different assumption in your will or living trust, with certain limitations that you should discuss with your attorney.

My wife, who is my main beneficiary, can use my life insurance proceeds to pay for my funeral expenses, right?

Not necessarily. Your life insurance company may not release the death benefit for many months, particularly if the cause of death seems unclear or suspicious. This is why it is important to anticipate any immediate financial needs. For example, how much money will your wife need to live each month? In the best-case scenario, you would create an emergency fund that would cover at least six months of living expenses and any death-related costs, and you would keep the fund in an account with a joint tenant with right of survivorship designation. Then, in the event that there is a delay in the release of your insurance proceeds, financial hardship will not be added to your wife's grief.

When my mother died, she left everything to me as the sole beneficiary. To help me out, the funeral director offered to process her life insurance and Social Security claims for an additional fee. Do you think this is a good idea?

The reason a funeral director would offer to perform these services for you is to make sure that the funeral costs will be paid as quickly and efficiently as possible—in other words, the funeral director is attending to his interests, not yours. Now, that doesn't necessarily mean the funeral director is dishonest, but I think the better way to handle this is to have the executor (or whoever is handling your deceased mother's affairs) make the life insurance and Social Security claims. The process will be better coordinated if one person handles all the claims.

I have a beloved dog who is like a member of my family. Can I leave her money after I die, so that I know she will be taken care of in the best possible way?

Most states consider pets your property, which means that they cannot receive property themselves or be the beneficiaries of a trust. Nevertheless, there are many passionate dog and cat owners who share your concern. A few states allow you to create a trust for the care of a pet, within certain limitations—including that the trust must terminate when your pet dies and that a court can reduce the amount of money in the trust if it feels you have set an excessive amount aside. Check with a local attorney to see if your state allows such a trust and whether it is appropriate for you. If there's someone you love and rely on who will be taking your pet after you die, you may just want to leave this person the money outright, with the understanding that he or she will use it to care for your dog.

As a beneficiary, if I inherit a house that still has a mortgage on it, will I get the house and mortgage as a package deal?

Probably. A will should be carefully drafted to avoid confusion about whether the person who is leaving you the house intends to pass the house on free and clear or subject to the mortgage. The promissory note and deed of trust held by the bank may require the mortgage be paid in full on the death of the mortgage holder. Be sure you know what the terms of the mortgage are before you take any action. And remember that even if the monies and the home are tied up in probate, any mortgage payments will still be due.

My father won't have much money when he dies, but he does own the house I grew up in free and clear. I know that it gives him a lot of comfort to know that, as his only beneficiary, I will be able to live in the house. Is a will adequate for him?

No, it is not! Let's think about what could happen to that house if your father passes it on to you through a will. You will have to pay probate fees. If your father has no other money that he is leaving you, you will have to pay those fees out of your own pocket immediately, before you can take ownership of the house. You might have to take out a loan in order to pay those fees. What if you do not qualify for a loan, and the only way you can pay the fees is to sell the house? These are choices you don't want to have to face, especially at a time when you are emotionally least equipped to do so. I'm sure this is not what your father would want for you. A revocable living trust, which I discuss later in this chapter, can eliminate probate fees. But please note: If there are estate taxes due on the house, you'll need to pay them whether your father had a will or a living trust.

GETTING A WILL

How do I make a will?

You can see an attorney to have a will drawn up, or you can write it yourself, if you are careful to fulfill certain requirements. You can also buy will forms from many bookstores and stationery stores (these are preprinted, with blank spaces where you write in the names of your beneficiaries and otherwise personalize the will), or you can buy computer software that will help you write a will. Many states now have a statutory will form that the state legislature has approved for use. This is the best choice if you are buying a form. You will see that preparing a will is relatively simple; it's after you die that the complications tend to arise. Still, keep in mind that any do-it-yourself will really needs to be reviewed by an attorney to make sure it is right for you. It probably won't include provisions to save on estate taxes or handle special situations—such as two families connected by a second marriage. And you'll need advice on title and beneficiary designations.

Can't I just write a will expressing my wishes on a regular piece of paper?

Yes. This is called a holographic will, and many states recognize it. If you decide to do this, you must write everything out in your own handwriting, date and sign the document, and then make sure that there is no other handwriting on the document—any marks in another person's handwriting will render your will invalid. If you make a mistake while you are writing a holographic will or change your mind after you have completed it, don't cross anything out, because that will also invalidate the will. Instead, tear it up and start over again. Be aware that a holographic will may ultimately turn out to be very expensive for your beneficiaries, since it is not unusual for special court hearings to be held to interpret what the will really says and to remedy omissions from the will. Contesting of the will may also be more common with a holographic will.

How much does a will cost?

If a lawyer draws up your will, it could cost between $100

and $3,000, depending on the complexity of your financial and personal situation and how much tax planning and drafting you require. A computer program costs about $50, and if you buy a will form at a stationery store it should cost less than $10.

Does a will have to be notarized?

No, but it needs to be witnessed when you sign it. Witnesses must be present to verify that you were of sound mind and weren't subject to undue influence or duress.

How many witnesses are required?

Most states require two, but some require three.

Can anyone witness my will?

Witnesses must be competent adults who are not named as a beneficiary or executor in the will. Remember, they simply need to be mature people who, if need be, could testify under oath that they watched you sign and that you did so by your own free will.

Do witnesses usually have to testify in court after someone dies?

Rarely, if ever. In fact, most states now have rules that allow witnesses to sign a brief affidavit at the time of witnessing declaring, essentially, that various signing formalities and requirements were followed. This means that, after you die, the will is "self-proving."

Do I have to reveal what's in my will to the witnesses?

No. All they are witnessing is that you are signing the will. As you sign, you tell them that what you are signing is your will, but they do not have to read it or be told anything about its contents.

Where to Keep the Will

I keep my will in my safe-deposit box. My sisters say that's a bad idea. Are they right?

Probably not. Although it's true that banks are capable of "sealing" a safe-deposit box after you die, this is not as common as it used to be. There are potential drawbacks, however. If your spouse or partner's name is not also on the box, and if no one has a key, it can be difficult for your loved ones to get access to your will after you die. Naming your children and spouse as joint tenants on the box or registering it in the name of your trust will make it easier for your successor, trustee, or loved ones to gain access to the box. The important thing is to keep your will in a place that you feel is safe. It can be your safe-deposit box, a home fire box, or the top drawer of your desk.

What if I have a safe-deposit box held in joint tenancy?

In this case, either joint tenant can open the box at any time, although in some states the box will be sealed after the death of one of the joint tenants, which means that the survivor will need a waiver or a government-approved inventory before gaining access to the box.

Changing Your Will

Can I change my will whenever I feel like it?

Yes, you can change your will at any time, for any reason. Call your attorney and ask him or her to draft a codicil, a separate document that incorporates your changes. My attorney prefers to rewrite the will, since it is easier to read a single document than to compare two separate documents and figure out which covers what topics. To avoid confusion later on, you should destroy any wills you have that are no longer valid. This is a good reason why you and you alone should hold all your original documents and not have them held for you by a lawyer (who may die, become disabled, retire, or move away).

Are there times when you can't change a will?
No, not unless you are mentally incapacitated or have signed another agreement that controls the contents of your will. The most typical examples of this might be a divorce decree or a prenuptial agreement, if you and your spouse (or maybe your ex-spouse on behalf of your children) have negotiated a specific bequest or other arrangement.

Instead of changing my will from time to time, couldn't I just leave everything to my estate?
Please do not do that, for remember, your estate will be distributed according to the last will that you had drawn up. If your will says your husband is to get everything and you have since divorced him and no longer want him to inherit your assets, he may still get everything upon your death if you don't change your will. If you do not have a will and you just leave everything to your estate, your assets will pass according to the intestate rules.

CONTESTS OF YOUR WILL

Can just anybody contest my will?

Relatives and others—creditors, significant others, those who gave you care—who think that they are entitled to a part of your estate can ask the court to award a share to them. The judge ultimately may not award the contestors anything, but your beneficiaries will have to wait during the probate until the claim is resolved, and they will need to spend some of your money fighting the claim.

Are there any circumstances in which my will is more likely to be contested?

The accepted grounds for contesting your will are that you were incompetent when you signed it and did not understand what you were doing, you were being pressured by someone to create a will that read a certain way and that he or she exerted undue influence on you, or there was some mistake made in the paperwork. It is not easy to win on any of these grounds. A will is most likely to be contested on the grounds of undue influence when one child is given considerably more or less than your other children or, if you are in a second marriage, your current wife or children from that marriage are given considerably more than you leave for the children from your first marriage. If you leave an unexpected bequest, such as to a lover or other individual whom your family does not know, there may be contests.

How can I discourage people from contesting my will?

Some attorneys advise that if you know someone may be hostile to your distribution plan, you leave him or her more than a token amount of money (not too large and not too small) as a bequest in the will and then include a "no contest" clause in the will. This means that a person contesting the will will receive nothing. The hope is that the person will be afraid of losing the bequest and so won't challenge the will. Such a bequest will probably cost your estate less than a court battle would, even if your intended beneficiaries won. Think of this bequest as an anti-contest insurance policy to protect your beneficiaries.

If you unintentionally omit a child or spouse from your will, however, the spouse or child can claim a share of your estate even if there is a no-contest clause. The law assumes that you would not intentionally exclude a spouse or child and will correct your "oversight" if it is challenged. This assumption covers even children born out of wedlock who you may not have known were yours! If you think there is even a remote possibility that you could have a child that you have not mentioned in your will, your attorney should include a special clause in the will called a pretermitted heir provision, which will make your intentions clear. However, state law may give your spouse or child a right to a portion of your estate no matter what.

A recent news item illustrates this seemingly farfetched point: A billionaire left his estate to his three known children. After he died, eight people from around the Pacific Rim made claims against the estate, saying that they were also his children and therefore rightful heirs. Their claims were initially denied in court. However, the man had had a biopsy done on a mole some years before he died and the doctor still had the sample. DNA from the sample was tested and, sure enough, all eight children were found to be his! Since the will had no pretermitted heir provision, they all were able to take shares equal to those of the other three children. The estate was divided into eleven shares.

Is there any way to completely prevent having my wishes contested?

No. You cannot prevent someone from going to court. However, if most of your property is transferred via a trust, you probably can minimize the possibility of having your wishes contested. Also, making an effort to clarify your wishes and decisions with your family, particularly if you are not leaving your children equal shares of your property, may abate potential confusion and resentment that could lead to a challenge. This could be as simple as a statement in your will or to your heirs reading, "I am leaving Jane half as much as I am leaving Cindy because Jane's income as an attorney is significantly higher than Cindy's as a nursery school teacher," or "John's bequest is larger than what I am leaving the rest of my children because he is disabled and has special expenses." The danger of putting in such explanations is what may happen in the event that Jane's earnings go down somewhat, or she stops working to be a stay-at-home mom, or she becomes disabled.

Wills and Relationships

Does a divorce automatically void a will that leaves property to a former spouse?

This is true in California, where I live, but is not automatically true in all states. Please don't make a mistake about this matter. The wishes you want to express in your will can be affected by a marriage, separation, or divorce, or even the birth of a child. When you experience a major life change of any kind, remember to review your will to be sure it still reflects your priorities and desires.

Another instance in which people often forget to review their wills or trusts is after a spouse or partner dies. In most cases, the deceased partner was designated to receive the bulk of the estate, so it's important to change your will or trust in this situation. While you're at it, don't forget to change the beneficiary on your IRA, 401(k), annuities, bonds, and life insurance policy, too.

What if I remarry and I die before changing my will to include my new wife?

Most states will award your new wife a share of your property, unless you have left her enough money via some other vehicle, such as a life insurance policy, or in a joint bank account, so that she is already receiving an amount equal to that to which a spouse is entitled under the intestate succession laws in your state. But don't rely on state laws. Take the time to revise and update your estate plan after this significant life change.

I'm in a second marriage, but I want to make sure that my children from my first marriage inherit my whole estate. How can I arrange this?

The first thing to do is to make sure that you have a will or a trust that expresses your wishes, because if you die without one, the rules of intestate succession will probably automatically entitle your current spouse to a specified portion of your estate. This is one area where you should definitely see an attorney. You will probably need a marital agreement with your second spouse specifying who owns income earned during the marriage. Also, be sure to avoid commingling of assets and to take title to your personal assets, keeping your goals in mind.

My wife and I drew up a will after our daughter was born, leaving everything to her after we're both gone. About ten years have passed, and we just realized that we've had two sons since then who aren't mentioned in our will! We're going to update it, of course, but what would happen if we died without doing so?

Your sons would probably be able to make a claim on your estate, but the probate court would control how much they could receive, and it would be a time-consuming and costly process for everyone involved, including the estate. They would also receive their entire share, probably at age 18, in one lump sum. This is another good reason to review and update your estate-planning documents regularly.

My son borrowed $30,000 from me for the down payment on his first house. He has been paying me back gradually but still owes me a lot. Are there any tax consequences if I forgive this debt in my will?

Yes, there are. Whether or not the loan was agreed to in writing, you are free to release your son from the obligation to pay you back. If you forgive the debt, however, you should know that the outstanding amount on the loan will be considered part of your estate for estate tax purposes. Also, the loan must be made at customary rates of interest. If you have charged only 2 percent interest when the standard rate is 8 percent, the IRS will say that you made a gift of the 6 percent difference. There are exceptions to this under so-called "gift loans." Get tax advice before forgiving debts in your will.

PROBATE

What is the point of probate, anyway?

Probate is an ancient process. It dates back to the feudal period in Europe. The reason for its existence today is essentially to make sure that an estate is distributed properly, according to the wishes of the deceased person. While this may be preferable to having no oversight process at all, the process involves expense, delays, and drawbacks. There are good alternative ways of controlling the distribution of your assets, mainly with a revocable living trust (more about trusts later).

How long does the probate period last?

The probate process can last anywhere from six months to two years or more.

I understand that my property won't formally be transferred while my estate is in probate. That's just a formality, right?

Wrong! It's not a formality to have your bank accounts under the jurisdiction of the probate court. While a spouse and minor children may be able to receive a family allowance during the probate process, allowances must generally be approved by a court. In the meantime, if your assets are not properly managed, or if the estate has to pay substantial fees while it is being managed, it could decrease significantly in value. Waiting too long to control what is rightfully yours is hardly a formality.

I recently saw a book in my local bookstore that was a collection of the last wills and testaments of famous people. Can just anyone learn the contents of any will?
This is something about probate that surprises a lot of people: Everything in your will becomes a matter of public record after the will has been probated. This means that anybody who can do a little research can discover the value of your estate. Even Jacqueline Kennedy Onassis, who was so protective of her privacy when she was alive, was not exempt from this—her will is available as a $4.95 paperback book! Unfortunately, it is not only the wills of the famous that are of interest: Some unscrupulous people regularly monitor all such records, because they are on the lookout for a person who's just inherited a chunk of money and might be vulnerable and gullible enough to invest in some scheme.

Do all states have probate?
Yes.

If I live in California but die while I am on vacation in Nevada, where will the probate take place?
Probate will take place in California, your primary state of residence—in legalese, the state of your domicile.

I am a single parent. Does the probate of my will concern only my financial affairs or could it affect my guardianship decision, too?
There are two types of guardianship: that of a person and that of an estate. The guardian of your child will control where the child lives and goes to school, give consent for medical treatment, and decide what religion the child will practice. The guardian of the estate will control the money. These guardians need not be the same person.

While the will is in probate, the court will establish a probate guardianship of the person. Typically, it will choose the guardian you selected, but it could, in certain circumstances, find that he or she is not in your child's best interest. It could also exercise control over any money your children are due to inherit until they turn 18. Trusts under a will or living trust can extend the payment date.

Keep in mind that the court will almost always appoint the surviving natural parent of a child as guardian, even if you had a terrible divorce and were granted sole custody of the child. If you are in this situation, you definitely want your child's money to be managed in a trust to prevent your former spouse from handling the child's money as the guardian of the estate.

THE COSTS OF PROBATE

How much does probate cost?

A lot! Your beneficiaries may have to pay court fees, attorneys' fees, and possibly even executor's fees. The total cost can range from about 4 percent of the total gross value of a large estate to more than 9 percent of a smaller estate, including the executor's fee. (The executor's fee may be waived, especially if the executor is the sole or main beneficiary.) Just as an example, in California, here are the fees you could expect to pay:

ESTATE SIZE	COMBINED BASIC FEES FOR EXECUTOR AND ATTORNEY
$100,000	$8,000
$200,000	$14,000
$300,000	$18,000
$400,000	$22,000
$500,000	$26,000
$600,000	$30,000
$1,000,000	$46,000

In states where there is no schedule of fees set forth by law, attorneys are free to charge whatever they like, subject to any agreement they make with you. If there is a small estate that takes a long time to settle due to unexpected details (and there are always unexpected details), the attorney can wind up charging a lot of money. In New Jersey, for example, a $70,000 estate left to your children could cost them $20,000 to probate! Keep in mind that these fees have to be paid before the remaining assets are distributed.

My mom and I live together in her home in California. A few years ago she took out a big mortgage to help with our expenses. Her house is worth $200,000, but she still owes about $190,000 on the mortgage. I plan to continue to live in it after she dies. How much will I owe in probate fees?

All states base probate on the fair market value of an asset, not on the equity in the asset. Because California law will calculate the value of the home without taking into account any loans taken against it, your mom's house would be valued at $200,000 for probate fee purposes. The same would hold true for cars or other assets your mother might still owe payments on. In this case, if all your mother owned was her house, the probate fees on it would be $10,300—more than the equity she has in the house.

What if I want to keep the house that was left to me, but I don't have the money to pay the probate fees?

Unless you can get a loan on the house, the house will be sold to pay the fees and you will be out of luck. Remember, when you go through probate, in most cases, the attorneys' fees are the first to be paid out of the estate. You avoid this with a trust.

My mother has Alzheimer's disease. Is it too late for her to get a living trust, or are we stuck with her will and going through probate?

It depends. State law may allow a judge to authorize establishment of a living trust as part of a court conservatorship or guardianship.

Can I save money by having my attorney serve as my executor?

In some states an attorney cannot take a fee for serving as the executor as well as the attorney for a probate estate. He or she must choose to be paid as one or the other. Although having a single person perform both jobs would, in theory, save you money, as a practical matter you won't find many attorneys willing to do both jobs. Some states see the double role as a conflict of interest and have laws that allow beneficiaries to prevent the attorney who wrote the will from acting as executor. Since some states go to such lengths to discourage this type of arrangement, it's generally not a good idea, unless the attorney is a relative or a close personal friend whom the beneficiaries are unlikely to find objectionable.

If an estate is going through probate, is there any way to reduce attorneys' fees?

You may be able to negotiate a lower fee. You can ask for a written agreement from the attorney stating that he or she will not charge extraordinary fees (which are in addition to the state-set statutory fees), or that such fees will not exceed a certain dollar amount.

Does the court charge a fee?

Courts charge a filing fee in order to accept a probate case. Most states require you to pay to have a notification of the death published in a newspaper for a period of several weeks. There are also recording fees, certification fees, and a fee for a court-appointed appraiser, who places a value on the estate. These various charges, which will differ depending on what state the deceased lived in and how much the estate is worth, can easily add up to several thousand dollars.

I've heard that I need to have my death published in a newspaper. Why would I need to do that?
Because it is required by law. The law exists to prevent fraud and to allow legitimate claims to be made against an estate. The small but significant possibility exists that an estranged relative or former business associate with whom you were on poor terms could read such a notice and decide to contest your will and seek a part of your estate or file a creditor's claim for money owed to him.

If it takes two years for my executor to probate my estate, will the estate have to pay income taxes on the money earned by the estate while it is still in probate?
Yes. This is something that many people overlook. An estate is like a person in that it must file an annual income tax return. It is the executor's responsibility to make sure the estate pays its taxes, and the executor is personally liable for the payment of the tax if the taxes aren't paid with estate funds. However, the executor is not liable if the estate had insufficient funds to pay the tax when the executor took over.

PROBATE ALTERNATIVES

Some states have begun to simplify their probate rules and procedures in certain circumstances (if, for example, you have a very small estate), allowing property to be transferred after someone dies by either an affidavit or a summary probate. If you're interested in pursuing this further, I'd recommend you check out *8 Ways to Avoid Probate*, published by Nolo Press.

What is a probate affidavit?

This is a legal form that certifies that your assets that would otherwise be subject to probate are worth less than a certain designated dollar amount. Your beneficiaries present this affidavit to the institutions that hold your assets, to show that they are legally entitled to them without a probate or court order.

How does the affidavit process work?

It simply requires whoever is going to own the deceased person's property to file an affidavit to transfer the title. Not all states will allow people to transfer real estate holdings in this way.

What is summary probate?

If the estate doesn't meet the requirements of a probate affidavit, some states might allow a summary probate, which means that the beneficiary petitions the court for immediate title to the estate's assets without the more formal probate process. An accounting is still required because, as with an affidavit, the estate has to be worth less than a value specified by the state to qualify for this special summary procedure. Owning real estate, though, does not generally disqualify you from a summary probate.

So you can't actually avoid the probate court with these procedures?

Not with summary probate—that always involves the court, albeit usually in a limited way and for a shorter time period. A probate affidavit avoids the court altogether.

If a person dies without a will, can you still use one of these less formal procedures?

If your state allows these alternative procedures, the state typically won't require that the deceased person have a will in order to implement them. There are, however, a few states that permit less formal procedures but require the deceased person to have authorized in his or her will the heir's use of them. A few others require all the beneficiaries of the will to consent to this procedure. Check with a local attorney specializing in trusts and estates about the situation in your state.

Which states have some form of a simplified probate procedure available?

It's actually simpler for me to tell you which states *don't* allow it: Connecticut, Delaware, Georgia, Louisiana, Mississippi, New Jersey, North Carolina, Rhode Island, and Washington.

How do you figure out whether an estate qualifies for this procedure?

The rules vary from state to state. Most states set a dollar figure, and generally the estate has to be quite small, sometimes smaller than $10,000 or $20,000. This usually means that you cannot use this type of probate alternative if you own any real estate other than raw land. As noted above, some states do not allow you to use these procedures if you own any real estate, no matter what it is worth.

Can you give me an example of an estate that would qualify for a probate alternative?

A typical example would be a person who either does not own a home or owns one jointly, whose bank account is under the statutory limit for a probate alternative or is held jointly, and who has beneficiary designations in place for retirement accounts.

How does the transfer of assets work through use of an affidavit?

If you are the beneficiary, you will simply give a certified copy of the affidavit, plus a copy of the death certificate and a copy of the will, if there is one, to, say, the Department of Motor Vehicles, if you are transferring title on a car, or to a bank, if you are transferring title to a bank account. There is usually a waiting period, such as 40 days from the date of death, to use these procedures.

TRUSTS

What is a trust?

A trust is a written agreement that sets forth who will manage the assets placed in it during your lifetime, in the event of your incapacity, and upon your death. It allows you to transfer the legal title of your assets to a trustee—either another person or yourself—and is often a more cost-effective alternative to a will.

What is a revocable living trust?

The most popular kind of trust is called a revocable living trust—"revocable" because you can change it at any time; "living" because you create and fund it while you are alive; and a "trust" because you entrust it with the title to your property.

The use of the term "living" to describe trusts has caused a lot of confusion among non-lawyers, so I'll try to offer a clear explanation on this point. Every trust is created while you're living. (The only exception is something called a testamentary trust, which is established after your death under the terms of your will.) The most significant fact about a trust is not whether it's "living" or not but whether it is revocable or irrevocable. Given that a revocable trust can be changed during your lifetime, it is the preferable choice in most instances.

Think of your revocable living trust as a suitcase into which you can put the title of your house, stocks, and other non-retirement-plan investments. You carry that trust with you while you are alive, with the ability to put new things in or take things out of it whenever you want. Everything in this suitcase is yours to own and enjoy the benefits from while you live. When you die, the suitcase is handed directly to your beneficiaries without passing through probate or any court. It's wonderfully uncomplicated, isn't it?

Another important aspect of a trust is that it provides for estate management in the event of incapacity. At this time, there are approximately 70,000 people alive in the U.S. who are 100 years of age or older. By the year 2050, this number is projected to be 835,000! When people reach their 80s or 90s, they can be quite vulnerable and aren't always capable of making decisions in their own best interest. The ability to choose who will manage your money if you are unable to do so, as well as who will decide when you should no longer be managing it for yourself, is a tremendous benefit of having a living trust.

How is a revocable living trust different from a will?

With a revocable living trust, you transfer title to your assets from your name as an individual to your name as trustee of your trust. (Married couples, especially those with separate property, have special issues.) Since all your property is in the name of the trust, when you die, your successor trustee has the immediate legal authority to sign over the assets held in the trust directly to the people you want to have them. Because your beneficiaries don't need to go to probate court in order to get your assets transferred to them, there won't be probate fees, and there will be no delays in transfer (except for the payment of death taxes and creditors); further, there may be no need for a public notice of death. Remember, the wishes expressed in your will can only be carried out with an order from the probate court. A revocable living trust will avoid this complicated and expensive process, although there are usually at least some attorneys' and accountants' fees to be paid.

Why would my property not be subject to probate just because it's in a trust?

The end result of probate is a court order signed by a judge that transfers the ownership of the assets from the deceased to the beneficiaries. With a living trust, you transfer title from your individual name into the name of the trust while you're alive, and you designate the beneficiaries who will receive the assets of the trust once you die. If you do this while you are alive, there is no need for the court to be involved in the transfer. No court, no probate. It really is that simple.

Think about it this way. Let's say my mother wants to leave me her home when she dies, and the deed to her home is in her name. She states in her will her wish that I inherit her house. Now, when she dies, I have a problem. Even though her will says the house is to go to me, how is it going to get into my name? She is no longer alive to sign the deed over to me. That's where the probate court comes in. A judge must approve the transfer. If my mother had left me the house in a living trust and had taken the step while she was alive to sign the deed of the house over to the name of the trust, then probate on the house would be avoided. If, however, she signed the trust but didn't sign a deed to put the house into the living trust, it would take a probate process to get the house into the living trust.

How does my revocable trust work when I die?

When you die, the successor trustee will take your death certificate and the trust documents to the bank, the brokerage house, the insurance company—any and all custodial institutions with assets held by the trust—and these institutions will change the title to the successor trustee's name. Subject to delays for appraisals, payment of debts, and the payment of estate taxes, the trustee will then sign the assets over to whomever they are designated to go by the trust documents—or, in some cases, will hold them in a new trust for the benefit of a minor child or for tax-planning purposes. If you hold real estate in a trust, a title company or lawyer will charge roughly $150 to prepare and record an affidavit of death of trustee and a new deed giving ownership to the beneficiaries. If the real estate is to be sold, an attorney, real estate broker, escrow company, or title company will do all the paperwork needed to transfer title as part of the sale.

If I have a revocable living trust, do I still need a will?

Yes. When you have a trust it is also essential that you have what is called a pour-over, or backup, will. Any assets not in your trust are "poured over" by your will. A pour-over will covers anything you might have left out of your trust by mistake. Basically, if your will states something like, "I leave the residue of my estate to the trustees of the Joe Smith Trust created by me on January 1, 1999," any assets not held in the trust are poured over into the trust by the will. The will also states any preference for a guardian, and expresses wishes about your memorial service and the disposition of your remains.

Defining the Terms

What is a trustor?

This is the legal term for the person who creates a trust and owns the property that has been put into the trust—namely, you. Sometimes a trustor is also referred to as the grantor or the settlor. When you create a trust, you may want to clearly claim certain rights that only you, as the trustor/grantor/settlor, have, such as the right to make changes in the trust.

What is a trustee?

This is the person or group of persons (or an entity such as a bank or a trust company, though I'd discourage you from using one of those) who controls the assets in the trust. Before you die, this person can be you. The trustee signs for and approves all the financial transactions of the trust. The trustee writes checks and makes investment choices for the trust, subject to the guidelines and provisions in the trust, and generally controls the trust's assets. If, after your death, your estate is distributed through a trust, the trustee that you named will distribute and sign over the assets according to what you have set up in the trust.

Is it advisable for me to be my own trustee?

Absolutely. The trustor, while he or she is alive, is usually the trustee. That's the great thing about a trust. You can continue to control everything as long as you are alive, and appoint a successor trustee to take over when you become incapacitated or die.

What is a successor trustee?

This is the person or entity who will succeed the original trustee when the trustee can no longer function in the capacity of the trustee, or no longer wants to. The conditions under which the successor trustee will step in should be spelled out in the trust document.

Does a trustee get paid?

Unless the trust agreement specifies otherwise, the trustee or successor trustee is entitled to compensation, based on how much in assets he or she is managing or in an amount that a court decides is "reasonable." If you have more than one trustee, there may be a separate fee for each trustee. Trustee compensation is one reason you want an attorney to look over your trust, to make sure that you have either arranged for an appropriate fee or have included a provision for your trustee(s) to waive it. Be wary of banks and financial institutions serving as trustees. They frequently charge between 1 and 2 percent of the asset value of the trust every year, or an even higher amount, as a minimum fee. In addition, they may charge transaction fees for selling and buying assets and then reinvest those assets in their own investment vehicles, making another commission. They are also more likely to seek court approval for routine trust matters that could be handled outside the court, thereby further increasing the administrative costs of the trust. Consider whether you want to require your trustee to obtain court approval for being paid in light of the expense incurred in such proceedings. In other words, select a trustee who has your and your beneficiaries' best interests at heart.

How much should my trustee be paid?

A trustee should be paid enough on an hourly basis so that the time spent administering the trust isn't a hardship. On the other hand, your trustee should not be profiting from the trust. Beware of the percentage fee.

If I am my own trustee, how should I choose a successor trustee?

A successor trustee must do three things. First, if you are disabled during your lifetime and unable to look after your own financial affairs, this person will manage them for you. Second, when you die, this person will locate your assets, pay your debts, file your taxes, and sign over the assets in the trust to the beneficiaries of your trust. Third, if there are beneficiaries who are minors, or others for whom you have continuing trusts as adults, the successor trustee will follow the trust's provisions on how to manage and invest the assets and make distributions for them until they are entitled to receive all the funds. In choosing a successor trustee, please consider all three functions. Remember, too, that the job of the trustee is not to act as a moneymaking machine. It is to be honest, to have your and your beneficiaries' best interests at heart, to be cognizant of your goals, and to be willing to seek help with things he or she doesn't understand. Someone who handles his or her own money in a responsible way is the best choice. On the other hand, be aware that people with demonstrated financial savvy will sometimes take greater risks than you would. The job of the successor trustee is, in essence, to carry out your intentions in the truest and most responsible way possible.

What is the principal?

The principal consists of the trust assets. Let's say you put 100 shares of Time Warner stock in your trust. The shares of stock are the principal. When the stock pays a dividend, the dividend is considered income. Trusts often make distinctions between how the principal and the income can be spent. In tax-planning trusts, there may be significant tax consequences based on how the trust describes the distribution of the income and principal. Make sure to ask your attorney if any limitations on spending are created by the language used in your trust.

What is a beneficiary?
A beneficiary is any person who benefits from the assets held in the name of the trust.

Can I be my own beneficiary?
Absolutely. You will almost certainly want to be the one who benefits from the assets in your trust while you are alive. In this case, you are the current beneficiary and whomever you designate to receive your property after you die will be the final beneficiary or beneficiaries.

WHO NEEDS A TRUST?

How do I know if I need a living trust?
Whether you need a living trust depends on the state in which you live, the size of your probate estate, and which assets you are leaving to your beneficiaries.

For smaller estates, there are three ways to avoid probate: probate affidavits and simplified court procedures, as well as POD, or payable-on-death, accounts, which I'll explain later. But if the assets you want to leave are larger than allowed for above, you should seriously consider a living trust. If you have a financial interest in a business, if you have children, if you are in a second or third marriage, if you are on bad terms with one or more of your heirs, if one of your family members is physically or mentally ill, developmentally disabled, in need of creditor protection, or just bad at managing money—you should seriously consider establishing a trust.

I always thought of trusts as primarily for rich people. Is that not true?

Sure, there are certain kinds of trusts expressly designed for people with a lot of assets, but revocable living trusts are very useful even if—especially if—your assets are more modest, because the less you have, the less you can afford to pay in probate fees.

Is it more important to have a trust if I have young children?

Yes. If you have young children for whom you want to provide asset management in the event of your death, you should seriously consider a living trust.

My sister says that she is leaving money for her young children to a custodian via a will. How is this different from a guardian? And would a living trust be better?

Some states allow you to make gifts or leave an inheritance to a minor by giving the gift or inheritance to a custodian who will hold, invest, and manage the property for the minor's benefit until he or she is old enough to care for it. (The state may require the child to take title of the property when he or she turns 18, 21, or 25.) Basically, a trust will allow you to do everything for your minor children that you could do by appointing a custodian, and will also let you retain greater flexibility and control. However, in some cases custodianships can provide a less expensive way to protect your children.

I am single and sold my house a few years ago and now my assets are in a couple of savings and retirement accounts. If I have more money than is allowed to qualify for a probate affidavit, do I need a revocable living trust?

Maybe not, since there is yet another way to avoid probate. Any account that has a designated beneficiary will not have to go through probate; it passes directly to the named beneficiary. One way to designate a beneficiary on your accounts is to ask your bank or brokerage firm to make your accounts payable on death (POD), which means that when you die the account balances will pass immediately to whomever you have identified as a beneficiary. Retirement accounts, such as IRAs, and insurance policies require you to designate a beneficiary on the application form, and those accounts will automatically avoid probate if you designate a beneficiary other than your estate. If you name your estate, however, your beneficiaries will have to go through probate. (That's because your estate is governed by your will, and wills typically have to go through probate.) To avoid probate, always name a person, not your estate, as beneficiary.

That said, I still think the best way to avoid probate is by setting up a trust. Let me explain. Let's say you have ten retirement accounts at ten different banks and brokerage firms. You want to change the primary beneficiary on each of these accounts. To do so, you must contact all ten institutions and fill out the required paperwork for each account, submitting a new form and providing necessary information about the person to whom you now want to leave your money. This is a lot of work. Alternatively, let's say the person you named as a primary beneficiary dies and you have not designated a contingent beneficiary. If you do not change the original beneficiary and you die, whether you wished it or not, your assets will go to the heirs of the deceased beneficiary. On the other hand, if you name your trust as the primary beneficiary and want to make a change, the process is easy. All you have to do is change one designation—that of the primary beneficiary of your trust.

One caveat, however, for married couples: Each of you

should always name your spouse as the primary beneficiary of your retirement accounts, and your trust as contingent beneficiary. For you, naming a trust as a primary beneficiary of IRAs or other retirement accounts may cause tax problems.

Remember, the main point of the revocable living trust is to avoid probate fees, save time, and designate a way to manage your assets in case of an incapacity.

If I spend part of the year in one state and part of the year in another, do I need a separate trust for each state?

No. Your trust should make clear which state law applies to the validity of the trust. This allows you to move, hold assets in different states, and not have to review or revise the trust based on a change of residence. Get legal advice as to whether a change of domicile requires changes to your plan if you are married or have children. If the trust is not clear on this point, then it will be governed by the law of the state of your domicile (your permanent state of residence). There are tests under the law to determine one's domicile.

If my spouse is not a U.S. citizen, do I need a trust?

While there is an unlimited marital deduction on estate taxes when one spouse inherits money from another spouse, if your spouse is not a U.S. citizen, the law sets a limit on the amount that can be inherited tax-free unless a special trust known as a QDOT is part of your will or living trust. In 2006, for example, the most a spouse who is not a U.S. citizen can inherit tax-free is $2,000,000 without a special trust. Consult an attorney, because the laws are complex.

If I have an interest in a business, is a living trust a good idea?

Yes. A living trust can be an excellent thing for you, especially if you want to protect the privacy of your business by keeping it out of probate. Your interest in the business can be transferred to the living trust without the court ever having to get involved. If you have business partners, you will probably need their permission in order to transfer title into the living trust, and you'll want to encourage them to set up their own trusts.

I've heard that a revocable living trust not only benefits my beneficiaries but also can help me during my lifetime. How so?

If you became incapacitated for any reason, your trust could make things much smoother for you, personally and financially. If you have an incapacity clause in your trust stating who can determine whether you should no longer be acting as trustee, the successor trustee can take over and protect you from yourself or others. This is one of the most important benefits of the trust.

Let me try to illustrate this with a worst-case scenario. Let's say you have a stroke and cannot sign your name. Without a living trust, in order for anyone, including you, to access your money (even to provide care for you), you would have to be declared incompetent in a court and have a conservator appointed for you. Each year, the conservator would have to prepare a statement accounting for every disbursement of your funds, as well as an assets-and-liability statement, and submit them to the court for approval. The conservator might also need to gain approval to buy or sell certain assets. A judge would then oversee all financial decisions made on your behalf.

If you already have a partner, friend, or relative whom you would trust to make these decisions, do you really want that person to have to go through this? The bottom line, in this scenario, is that you would have to pay unnecessary attorney and court fees to establish and continue the conservatorship and permit a judge whom you don't know to control your finances. If you have an incapacity clause in your revocable living trust, you maintain some control in this situation, because your wishes are likely to be followed, without going through the court.

Can I name someone in my will to take over my financial affairs if I become incapacitated, or can I only do this with a trust?

A will expresses your wishes to the court only after you die. If you have not made arrangements in case you became incapacitated (through a living trust or a durable power of attorney for asset management, which we'll discuss later), your loved ones would have to go to court to establish a conservatorship. That means they would have to prove your incompetency in order to gain control over your financial affairs. This is a time-consuming, unpleasant, and expensive process.

The importance of making provisions in such circumstances simply cannot be emphasized enough. After age 65, almost half of the population will spend an average of two years and nine months of their lives unable to care for themselves due to a physical or mental incapacity. It is a sobering statistic, without a doubt, and what it suggests is enormously unpleasant for us personally, though no less important if we choose to ignore it.

Let's say that you are in your 80s and starting to have a bad time with numbers, and you have made some poor investment decisions. Your spouse and children can see that something is wrong, but you are not "incompetent," as that term is defined by the law: You can still get dressed by yourself, care for your basic needs, and tell people what you want. In this case, you would be found not to be in need of a conservator. Meanwhile, you could lose all your money and leave your spouse penniless. However, if you had a trust or a power of attorney, then your successor trustee or agent could manage your funds for you. With a trust, you could grant those closest to you financial control and keep the courts out of it.

I have personally seen this very situation unfold several times. One of the first signs of Alzheimer's disease is difficulty remembering numbers, which can affect your investment decisions. Often, however, it is weeks or months before an authoritative diagnosis is made, even though your loved ones already know that something is wrong because they know you. A trust allows action to be taken when it's necessary to take action, and before it is too late.

The living trust sounds good, but it sounds like something I don't need to think about until I have had a chance to accumulate some assets. Right?

Wrong as can be. Even if you haven't had a chance to accumulate significant assets, you should still think about creating a living trust. Also, you may have more assets than you think: For example, if you have young children and have purchased a term life insurance policy to protect them, a living trust can best help you preserve as much of that money for them as possible by deciding who will oversee those funds for them, avoiding reports and accountings to a court.

Is there anyone who should not have a trust?

If you own only raw land as your real estate, your state might have a procedure called informal administration or a probate affidavit, which allows you (depending on the size of your estate) to pass assets on without going through the formal court probate process. Also, if you are in the process of applying for Medicaid, or think you will do so within five years, you should probably not be setting up a trust. If you are in this position, you need to consult a good attorney with some expertise in elder care and Medicaid eligibility in your state.

This all sounds fine, except that I don't want to have a penny left when I die. If I'm trying to spend it all while I'm alive, I don't need to worry about trusts, do I?

That might be true, but what if you die unexpectedly in a car accident before you've spent all your money? Or if you're seriously injured and don't die immediately? In cases such as these, you would still need to take responsibility for decisions about your health care and your financial affairs.

Setting Up a Revocable Living Trust

How do I set up a revocable living trust?

A certain amount of paperwork is required in order to set up and fund a trust. As with a will, you can have an attorney draw up the trust document for you or you can use a book or computer program to write one yourself. I recommend that you have an attorney draft it. If you do write it yourself, have an attorney look it over and make sure you have done it correctly. Once you've created the document and signed it, you need to transfer the ownership (the legal title) of almost all your assets (get legal advice on what not to transfer) into the name of the trust to avoid probate and to allow a successor trustee to act on your behalf in case of incapacity. This last step is known as funding the trust. You must fund the trust after it is created for the trust to take effect.

How much will it cost to set up a trust?

You'll want to ask your attorney about this up front, and you should not accept a vague answer. Any experienced attorney who knows the size of your estate, the assets you own, and the type of planning required should be able to give you a written agreement on the cost of setting up the trust. I prefer that you have someone bill you on a project basis, which means that he or she will charge you a flat fee for the cost of drawing up your trust and funding it for you, rather than bill you on an hourly basis. That way, if setting up your trusts takes the attorney longer than anticipated, this misjudgment will not cost you money.

In California, a simple revocable trust for an individual—for example, one that takes into account a piece of property and a few basic bank accounts, calls for outright distributions for beneficiaries (not complicated trust arrangements), and does not include any tax planning—should cost between about $1,500 and $2,000. Be wary of anyone who charges you only a few hundred dollars, or anything significantly below market rates. He or she probably will not be able to spend an adequate amount of time researching your situation or explaining it to you, and may charge extra for services that should be included, such as funding the trust.

How do I decide what assets to leave to whom?

Everyone's family is different, and so is everyone's idea of what is fair. In light of this, your first step is to decide what your own objectives are. If you are currently helping to support an elderly parent, for example, then you won't want to forget that parent in your trust; you'll want to continue to provide for him or her in case you die before he or she does. If, on the other hand, leaving assets to your parents will only increase their estate and create estate tax problems, you should bypass their estate. (There are ways to benefit your parents through carefully designed trusts that will not be taxed in their estates. An estates attorney can help you find one that's right for you.) There are many ways to benefit a spouse through a trust, but a lot of them have tax implications and should be discussed with an attorney. You may also want to discuss trusts for your children. Don't forget to consider what you would want to have happen if one or more of your children predeceased you, or if your children died before you did and left no grandchildren. At this point, there might be a charity or friends that you would rather name as your beneficiaries than distant relatives.

The most difficult issues in naming beneficiaries seem to arise when there are children from different marriages. If you have two children, for example, and your husband has one, don't be surprised if he feels unhappy when you suggest that everything be split in three equal shares. He may believe that one half of your shared assets is his and should go to his child and the other half is yours and should go to your two children. Without a doubt, stepparent relationships can pose challenges. You'll need to make some indication in your trust about these matters to avoid confusion. Be ready to compromise if need be. Also, beware of making children too financially independent—the pitfalls of such arrangements should be obvious to you.

How important is it to review my beneficiary designations once I create a trust?

It's very important. Many years ago, a woman I knew got divorced from her husband of 30 years. Recently, she died. Because she never reviewed the trust she had set up while she was married, she left everything to her ex-husband. Since many people hold significant assets within a trust, it is crucial to review the beneficiary designations as your life situation changes.

How often should I review my trust to update it?
If your revocable living trust is simple, with no estate-tax planning, you may never have to make any changes in it unless there is a major change in your circumstances or relationships. Even if circumstances do change, your trust may last a lifetime if it has been properly written and you have been guided through all the contingencies by your attorney. For example, if one of your beneficiaries dies before you, there should be a provision in the trust to meet that contingency.

I set up a trust a number of years ago when I lived in Colorado. Do I have to change it now that I have moved to Arizona?
Most likely you won't have to change your trust just because you have moved to a new state, though your trust documents should say which state's laws govern it. You should consult an attorney in your new state to see whether your trust will need to be revised.

I thought you couldn't make changes to a trust. Am I wrong?
Whether or not you can change a trust depends on whether the trust is revocable or irrevocable. Remember, revocable means that you can make changes whenever you want to. In fact, it can be easier to make changes to a revocable living trust than to a will, because you don't need two witnesses to authenticate your signature (although you usually want your signature notarized to avoid disputes as to whether you were the one who signed the document). An irrevocable trust, usually used for advance tax-planning purposes or after you become incapacitated or die, cannot (except under special circumstances) be changed once it's created.

How is a trust terminated?

Your trust agreement will have a provision that states how or when your trust can be terminated. For example, a grantor can create a trust to last for 20 years, or until his or her youngest beneficiary turns 35 or dies, whichever comes first. A beneficiary usually may not terminate a trust on his own, unless it's specifically permitted by the trust agreement. If you are concerned about someone terminating the trust too soon, make sure that you express your intentions clearly in the trust agreement. A court will try to honor your intentions if it knows what they are.

FINDING A GOOD LAWYER

How can I find a reliable trusts and estates attorney?

The best method of finding an attorney is by word of mouth. If your friends or relatives have found an attorney they like who is a specialist with trusts and estates, check that person out. See the Additional Resources section for information about how to locate an estate attorney.

How do I know if my lawyer is up to par? What should he or she do for me in exchange for the fee I'm paying?

It's important that the attorney you are going to rely on to help you organize the financial future of your family have at least ten years of experience with wills, trusts, and estate planning. He or she should ideally have drafted at least 200 wills and trusts before drafting yours. And you and your family should be comfortable with him or her.

Since the attorney probably already has a boilerplate trust agreement that he or she will fill in with your particulars, preparing the document should not account for the bulk of the fees. Ask whether the attorney will be drafting the documents himself, but don't worry if an associate will be doing the paperwork, as long as that person is properly supervised. (The cost to you may be less if an associate does the work.) You do want to know exactly what you will be paying for. To that end, get an agreement in writing stating what services you will receive and how much the attorney will charge for them, including any charges for calling him with questions. (If your questions do not exceed the time limit spelled out in your agreement with him, you shouldn't be charged.)

What you are really paying for is the time your attorney will take to review your situation and explain everything about your documents and how your trust will work. Among the things he or she should do for you are: review your deeds and title documents to look for past mistakes; ask you questions about estate planning issues that you may not have considered; and create a plan for your individual situation, encompassing your financial goals. He or she should also review your beneficiary designation forms on your IRAs, Keoghs, annuities, and life insurance policies and bring them up to date.

While creating your trust, your attorney should be thinking about your overall interests and asking you questions about estate planning issues, including long-term care insurance, health care, durable living powers of attorney, gifting programs, and/or any charitable preferences you have. After all, what's the point of drawing up a trust to protect your assets if someday you have to use them to pay long-term care costs?

Once the trust is set up, your attorney should fund it for you, changing the title of the appropriate assets from your individual name to the name of your trust and adding your beneficiary designations. This is crucial. Without the funding component, you have wasted the money you spent to create the trust.

Finally, for the single project fee, I would like to see your attorney draft a backup will and a durable power of attorney for your health care.

Why does my lawyer think that I don't need a revocable living trust?

Do you remember those probate fees I mentioned earlier? Well, they get paid to your executor and to your attorney. So, in most states, attorneys stand to profit from your having only a will and not a revocable living trust. This may explain why your attorney has told you that you don't need one.

Also keep in mind that your attorney may not be an estate specialist and may not be familiar with all the benefits of trusts. Ask him how many trusts he has written in the last three months and how many allocation agreements for A-B trusts he has prepared. If he looks at you as if you're speaking Greek, politely get up and leave.

To prove the point, I want you to ask your attorney to estimate for you, in writing and on his or her letterhead, the following:

1. How much it would cost you to have a will drawn up, if you don't already have one;
2. How much it would cost your beneficiaries to probate your entire estate (including court costs and attorney and executor fees) if you and your spouse died today with wills alone;
3. How much it would cost to create and fund a revocable living trust; and
4. How much it would cost your beneficiaries to settle your estate if you and your spouse died today with that revocable living trust.

Add the cost of drawing up each document to the respective cost to your beneficiaries after your death and compare the two totals. The option that costs less is the one your attorney should recommend. If the calculations suggest that you would be better off with a trust, and you've been told it's unnecessary, you may need to get a new attorney.

If the calculations suggest that you do not need a trust and your attorney can clearly explain this to you, be sure to review your financial status and the relevant laws every few years to be sure that having only a will still makes sense for you.

FUNDING THE TRUST

How do you fund a revocable living trust?

Funding a trust means transferring ownership of certain assets into the trust while you are still alive. The process can be as simple as changing title to an asset like a bank account, or it can involve preparing a new deed and recording it, depending on the types of assets you will be holding in the trust.

Do I have to fund (transfer assets into) my revocable living trust?

If you don't fund the trust, your trust will be nothing more than a document stating who gets what. In other words, it is "empty." If you die with an "empty" trust, your beneficiaries will have to go through probate with your will in order to get your assets into the trust.

Which assets belong in my trust?

Real estate, bank accounts, stocks, bonds, investment accounts, partnership interests, the stock in your family corporation, and credit union accounts.

Be careful how you record any deeds for real estate, because correcting mistakes once a deed has been recorded may be very difficult. Have your attorney or a title company prepare and record your deeds. Be careful, too, of including assets that are tax shelters. If you move those assets to the trust, such a transfer may be considered a change of ownership, which means you lose the tax advantage. Finally, accounts that designate a beneficiary—such as life insurance, annuities, employee benefits, incentive stock options, IRAs, Keoghs, and other pension plans—will continue to be owned by you rather than by the trust, but the trust can be named the primary or contingent beneficiary, depending on the asset. Get tax advice before making any transfers or changing any beneficiary designations.

Except for life insurance, incentive stock options, retirement plans, and the like, should I put everything I own into a revocable living trust?

Yes. I recommend putting in everything as outlined above, including personal property. Personal property includes household items, jewelry, cars, tools, computers, clothing, and anything else without legal title.

After the trust is funded, will my name still be on the titles to my property?

Yes. If you originally owned your house as Mary Smith and you have created a revocable living trust, the title will have been transferred so that the house now belongs to "Mary Smith, trustee for the Mary Smith Revocable Living Trust." And when a new deed for any real estate you own is prepared and recorded, it might say, for example, that Mary Smith grants all her interest in the property to Mary Smith as trustee of the Mary Smith Trust, dated 1-1-01. The naming process will apply to bank accounts, brokerage accounts, mutual funds, partnership and business interests, stocks, and more.

After the trust is funded, will I be giving up control of any of my assets by changing the titles in this way?

Not at all. You can retain complete control and management over all your assets for as long as you are alive, willing, and able to handle your own financial affairs. That means that nothing can be done without your signature. If you resign as trustee, become incapacitated, or die, the successor trustee you have named will become the new signer for the trust.

After I fund my trust is there any difference between owning my bank accounts as an individual and owning them within the trust?

The only possible difference concerns the $100,000 FDIC protection on savings accounts. If you and your spouse each have $100,000 in savings, normally you would each be protected for that amount. If your assets are combined in a trust, however, some banks will only insure the trust for up to $100,000. Check with your bank.

What about my house—should I be aware of any differences once I put it in the trust?

Some banks may not be willing to refinance your house while it is in a trust for the simple reason that they don't want to pay an attorney to read the trust. If you encounter this, it is a simple matter to transfer the title to your house out of the trust and into your name as an individual, and then to transfer the title back to the trust after the refinancing is completed. A title company and/or your attorney can assist you with this for a modest fee.

TRUSTS AND DEBTS

How will the trust work if I die and still have debts to be paid off?

In all cases, debts are paid according to a priority list designated by your state—for example, funeral expenses and taxes, then the cost of administration of the estate, family allowance, etc., until finally all legitimate debts are paid off.

Will a trust protect my assets from creditors?

This is a common question. A revocable trust is considered a "transparent" trust, which means that creditors can reach it, as long as the creator of the trust is also a beneficiary of the trust. The simple answer is that, in most cases, the assets are not protected.

TRUSTS AND RETIREMENT ACCOUNTS

Should I make my revocable living trust the beneficiary of my retirement accounts?

This depends on whether you are married or single and on the proper tax advice for your situation. If you are not legally married, you may want to name the trust as the primary beneficiary. If you are married, you should name your spouse as the primary beneficiary, and you may want to name the trust or a subtrust as the contingent beneficiary. The reason for this is that spouses have specific rights regarding retirement proceeds that are highly beneficial tax-wise, and you don't want to lose those tax advantages. The reason you may want to name your trust as the contingent beneficiary is so that, if you make a change in the trust, you won't have to change all your contingent beneficiary designations; they are keyed to the trust. A change in the trust automatically changes all the beneficiary designations.

Trusts and Relationships

Should I have the same person act as the guardian for my children, the executor of my estate, and the trustee of my revocable living trust?

Most people appoint their spouse or partner to all three positions. (You should also think about what would happen if both you and your partner were to die.) Generally, it will simplify things greatly if one person has control over everything, as you do now. But you will have to decide whether the person you want to raise your children is also the best person to make financial decisions for them. If there are different people in your life who would bring different skills to benefit your children, you may want to appoint different individuals to each position. Just make sure that the people you appoint will be able to work comfortably with one another for as long as your children will need them.

I have been told that if my children are still young it is a good idea to appoint a professional trustee. Is this true?

No. I wouldn't recommend a professional trustee unless there is absolutely no one else who can serve in that role. Professional trustees are expensive and may not necessarily manage assets well. It is critical that the person you choose to act as your trustee be honest, trustworthy, and able to communicate with your beneficiaries, because he or she will have a great deal of discretion in the management of your affairs. If I were you, I would look to a friend or relative who is capable of filling the role.

One of my children has a substance abuse problem. I don't want to disinherit her, but I'm worried about her ability to manage money responsibly. What's the best option for me?

This is the perfect example of how a discretionary trust under a will or living trust can be beneficial. With a trust under a will or living trust, you can arrange for your daughter to receive a small but consistent amount of income over time rather than a lump-sum inheritance.

Is it possible to disinherit your spouse or your children?

It depends on state law. If you're married, a prenuptial agreement may control the result.

Can I put a condition on my bequests, such as that I want to give my daughter money only if she marries?

Theoretically, yes, in which case you would be making what's called a "conditional gift." The state you live in may refuse to enforce your condition if it would cause your daughter to do something illegal or against public policy. An example of this would be if you said you would give your daughter a gift only if she converted from her current religion. Such a condition is against public policy, so your daughter would be entitled to the gift anyway. Before you are tempted to complicate your bequests in this way, please think carefully about why you are trying to control your daughter from the grave and whether your wishes are truly in her best interest.

TRUSTS AND INCOME TAX

Is having a revocable living trust going to complicate my tax returns?

Not at all. You need not file an income tax return for a revocable trust of which you are the trustee. You simply file a regular tax return as you always do. There are no special income-tax-reporting consequences during your lifetime.

Are there any income tax benefits to establishing a revocable living trust?

No. The main purpose of having a living revocable trust is to avoid probate after your death and to help with the management of your affairs in case of incapacity.

If I sell my house after I have transferred it to my revocable living trust, can I still take advantage of tax benefits I would have received if I had sold it as an individual?

Absolutely. The sale will take place in the same way that it would without the trust, and you will be able to claim the income tax benefits as the grantor of the trust. (The tax result may be different if you're married, the house is sold after one of you dies, and some or all of the house is held in certain trusts.)

If I am still working when I die, would I owe income taxes for that year?

Yes, you would. Your executor or trustee will be responsible for filing an individual income tax return for you, a separate tax form for your estate, and, if the estate is large enough, a federal estate tax return.

The executor or trustee may not file the final tax return until the year following the death. Since the return will be marked "deceased," this is an invitation for the IRS to review the previous three years of tax returns; they know they won't get another chance. (The IRS has three years from the date of a filing to challenge it.) Because the executor or trustee can be personally liable for the payment of taxes, you want to be sure that the trust holds in reserve an amount sufficient to pay any back and/or current taxes. The IRS reviews every estate tax return that is filed, and it audits approximately one out of every ten. The IRS will send you a letter, usually within a year of the filing, saying it has received the return and has no current plans to challenge it. However, until the three-year period has passed, the agency may initiate an audit at any time.

Estate Taxes

For many people, one of the most important things to know when considering estate-tax planning is that married spouses can leave each other as much money and property as they like without the surviving spouse owing any estate tax. This is called the unlimited marital deduction and is a significant benefit of being married. But for single people, unmarried partners, and married people concerned about leaving assets to children and others, serious planning may be in order.

What is estate tax?

Although recent legislation has passed eliminating the federal estate tax as of 2010, at the time of this writing estate taxes are federal taxes that are owed nine months after death on the net value of a taxable estate if it is worth more than a specified amount. The net value of an estate is determined by adding up the gross value of your stocks, bonds, bank and investment accounts, real estate or other jointly held property, life insurance proceeds, retirement accounts (IRAs, pension funds, or Keoghs), personal property, and any other assets you leave behind, and subtracting from that amount the costs of your funeral, your debts, any administrative expenses, and any assets that you leave to your spouse or a qualified charity (in a manner approved by the IRS). What's left is subject to estate taxes, if the amount exceeds that allowed for the year in which you die.

Please note that estate tax has always been distinct from probate fees and state inheritance taxes, both of which vary by state. It is also distinct from income tax, which you pay on personal income every year.

How much can you pass on to beneficiaries before they owe estate tax?

Right now, depending on the year in which you die, your taxable estate is subject to federal estate tax if it exceeds:

2006–2008	$2,000,000
2009	$3,500,000
2010	No estate tax
2011	$1,000,000 (unless Congress extends repeal)

These exempt amounts can be reduced by lifetime gifts above the annual federal gift-tax exclusion.

Are these figures a kind of tax deduction?

That is a common question. These figures are called "unified credits" and they actually do function as a deduction of sorts, by zeroing out the tax up to the amount shown for a given year. This means that the value of your estate will be calculated in full, but you will already have a credit for the amount of estate tax that would have been "owed," for example, on the first $2,000,000 if you died in 2006.

What are the rates of estate taxes?

As of 2006, basically anything over the exemption amount will be taxed at 46 percent. (The highest estate tax rates have changed. See page 68.) There are other special estate tax rules and even another type of federal estate tax, the generation-skipping transfer tax. With such substantial tax owed on estates over the exemption amount—and since estate tax is due within nine months of your death—you can imagine the potential problems for your heirs: They could be forced to sell off some of your assets at less than their optimal value in order to meet tax obligations.

Are there ways to reduce my estate tax?

You reduce your estate taxes whenever you reduce the value of your taxable estate. There are a number of ways to do this. You can give gifts of $12,000 (as of 2006) to as many people as you like each year without incurring a gift tax. You also can pay another person's college tuition in any amount each year and it will not be subject to gift tax, even if it's more than $12,000. But if you do this, you must be sure that the check is made out directly to the school and not to the student. You

CALENDAR YEAR	ESTATE AND GST TAX DEATHTIME TRANSFER EXEMPTION	HIGHEST ESTATE AND GIFT-TAX RATES
2006	$2 million	46%
2007	$2 million	45%
2008	$2 million	45%
2009	$3.5 million	45%
2010	N/A (taxes repealed)	top individual rate under the bill (gift tax only)
2011	$1 million (unless Congress extends repeal)	55%

Source: Joint Committee on Taxation

may also pay medical expenses for another person in any amount if you pay them directly to the medical provider, and the money will not be subject to gift tax. If you own a home, you may gift that home in a qualified residence trust and receive a substantial discount in the way the home is valued for estate tax purposes. (Please note, there are many complications and risks with this type of trust.)

How does the IRS determine how much the estate is worth, since some of my assets may change in value over time?

Generally, the value of your estate is established according to its fair market value on the day you die. Alternatively, your executor can choose a date exactly six months from the day of your death, if doing so will result in a lowering of your estate tax. These are the only two dates that can be used.

Is estate tax due before my will is probated or after my beneficiaries receive their assets?

Federal estate tax is due nine months from the date of death, regardless of whether the estate is in probate or its assets have been distributed to heirs. Sometimes it is possible to arrange to make a series of smaller payments—if, for example, you have a family-owned business that would incur great hardship if it had to pay an estate tax in one lump sum. But please note that, in most cases, this money is due and payable in full within nine months.

What happens if the executor doesn't file a federal estate tax return within the mandated time period?

It could get expensive. If the executor doesn't have a good reason for having failed to file the return, the estate could owe a fine of 5 percent of whatever tax is due for each month that the tax return is late, up to a maximum of 25 percent of the tax bill. This is yet another reason to choose a responsible executor.

You mentioned earlier that federal estate tax is separate from state inheritance tax. Which states charge separate inheritance taxes?

Indiana, Iowa, Kentucky, Maryland, Nebraska (county inheritance tax only), New Jersey, Ohio, Oklahoma, Pennsylvania, and Tennessee all charge inheritance taxes. Sometimes these are called death taxes.

How do the state inheritance taxes work?

Every state is different, but, as of 2006, here's the general idea: Until recently, most states did not impose their own estate tax. Instead, they had what is known as a "pickup tax" that let them take a share of the federal estate tax paid by large estates. But with the phaseout of federal estate taxes, states don't get a share of federal estate tax anymore. To recoup some of that loss, some states are collecting tax from estates that are not big enough to owe any federal tax. In New Jersey, Rhode Island, and Wisconsin, for example, estates worth more than $675,000 may owe estate tax. (Surviving spouses still get a break; property left to them is exempt from state estate tax, just as it is exempt from federal estate tax.)

Some states have additional inheritance taxes—again, as of 2006. Unlike estate taxes, which depend on how large your taxable estate is, inheritance taxes are calculated on what each beneficiary receives. Inheritance tax rates will depend on the closeness of the relationship of the beneficiary to the decedent. Distant relatives or unrelated persons pay more than spouses or children. In most cases, you will not pay more in state taxes than what you are assessed in federal taxes.

How are state estate taxes affected by the federal phaseout of the tax in 2010?

While states have previously tied their estate tax to federal tax by taking a portion of the federal tax owed, many states have moved to "decouple" their tax from the federal levy. That's because states are looking at severe revenue shortfalls and do not want to be caught losing out on potential revenue from now until 2010, when the federal estate tax is scheduled to disappear for that one year. Basically, that "decoupling" involves the states declaring that their estate-tax rules will not be tied to the new federal rules, but instead will be tied to the old laws as they existed before the changes began to take shape in 2001.

Which states have decoupled, and what are the new rules I should know if I live in one of those states?

As I am writing this in late 2006, 17 states that levied pickup taxes prior to 2001 have retained estate taxes, either by decoupling or replacing their pickup taxes with estate taxes not tied to the federal tax. They are: Illinois, Maine, Maryland, Massachusetts, Minnesota, Nebraska, New Jersey, North Carolina, Rhode Island, Vermont, Wisconsin (decoupled through 2007), Kansas, New York, Connecticut, Oregon, Virginia, and Washington, as well as the District of Columbia.

The rules and regulations vary from state to state and are quite complicated. I advise anyone in a state mentioned above who has an estate valued at more than $675,000, to seek professional advice on how best to construct an estate plan that takes into account changes in state laws. In the Additional Resources section at the end of this volume, you will find information on the American Academy of Estate Planning Attorneys.

Are things that don't go through probate, such as a life insurance policy, subject to estate taxes?

Generally, yes. Remember, retirement accounts, life insurance, property held as joint tenants with right of survivorship, and retirement benefits will all avoid the delays and fees of probate but still will most likely count toward calculating your taxable estate. However, you can set up a life insurance trust or make other arrangements that could keep the life insurance proceeds out of your taxable estate.

If my life insurance proceeds go to my designated beneficiary, why does that amount count toward the assets of my estate for tax purposes?

I'm glad you asked this question, because insurance agents love to say that life insurance is tax-free, and this is a misleading statement. While it is true that your heirs won't have to pay income tax on these benefits, if you are the owner of the policy and you control the right to designate its beneficiary, the proceeds will be considered an asset to be included in your estate, and taxed accordingly, when you die. As mentioned earlier, there are ways to exclude life insurance from estate tax.

So my retirement account is subject to income taxes and estate taxes?

Yes, if you have a traditional IRA or employer-sponsored retirement plan, you will owe income tax on the value of the account and it also may be subject to estate taxes after you die. If it is subject to estate tax, you may get an income tax deduction. Roth IRAs are subject to estate tax, but not to income tax if all the requirements are met.

Can I avoid estate taxes altogether?

Here is where married people have a big advantage: You will not owe estate taxes on property that you leave to your spouse, as long as your spouse is a U.S. citizen. (Your spouse's beneficiaries, however, may end up owing estate tax on these assets after your spouse's death.) Another option to consider is to create an A-B trust, which I'll explain a little later.

GENERATION-SKIPPING TAX

Is estate tax the same as the generation-skipping tax?

No. The generation-skipping tax is an additional tax, on top of any estate tax, that applies to any portion of your taxable estate more than $2,000,000 (for 2006) that you transfer to a grandchild or grandchildren while your own child is still living, or to anyone else who is two or more generations younger than you are (as of 2001). The generation-skipping tax is not a per-beneficiary exemption. It's a per-transfer exemption of up to $2,000,000 (for 2006—for other years see the chart below).

For 2006, anything above that left to grandchildren is taxed at a flat rate of a whopping 46 percent. The generation-skipping tax is meant to keep affluent families from passing on assets without having to pay taxes, but it will be repealed as of the year 2010.

GENERATION-SKIPPING TRANSFER TAX RATE

YEAR	RATE	TAXED ON AMOUNT THAT EXCEEDS
2006	46%	$2,000,000
2007	45%	$2,000,000
2008	45%	$2,000,000
2009	45%	$3,500,000

Does this mean that if I left money to my granddaughter, she would owe this tax, but if I left it to my daughter, she wouldn't?

Yes, if the gift is very large and if you leave it before the year 2010. This is the point: If your daughter were to receive money from you and then left that money to her own daughter, the government would theoretically be entitled to tax the money twice, once upon your death and once upon your daughter's death. If your granddaughter receives the bequest directly, the money is subjected to estate tax and the generation-skipping tax because you have "skipped" her mother. So, in effect, the transfer is still being taxed twice. You shouldn't be too concerned about this tax, since the first $2,000,000 (for 2006) that you transfer directly to your granddaughter is exempt from it, though not, of course, from estate tax. (Married couples can exempt up to a combined $4,000,000 [for 2006].) If you intend to pass on more than that amount of money or property to your grandchildren, you should consult an attorney. There are other types of exemptions and trust plans that are designed to preserve as much of your estate as possible.

My daughter has predeceased me, and her sons are my beneficiaries. It doesn't seem fair that my grandsons will have to pay the generation-skipping tax on what I leave them, when I couldn't leave anything to my daughter.

Don't worry. There are a number of exceptions to the generation-skipping tax, and this is one of them. In this case, the law allows you to leave assets to the children of your deceased child as if they were your own children.

What about the $12,000-per-year gift rule—does that count toward the $1,000,000 exemption on the generation-skipping tax?

No. If you give your granddaughter $12,000 each year, the accumulated funds will not be subject to the gift tax or the generation-skipping tax, and you do not need to apply that gift to the exemption for the generation-skipping tax.

A-B Trusts

An A-B trust (also known as a tax-planning trust, a credit shelter trust, a marital trust, or a bypass trust) is a single trust made while both spouses are alive. When one spouse dies, the trust is normally split into two shares, an A share and a B share. (Sometimes there are three shares: A, B, and C.) One share remains a revocable trust, and the other becomes an irrevocable trust. You can create an A-B trust through a revocable living trust or through a will.

A-B trusts should be considered if you are married and have

assets in excess of the nontaxable exemptions amounts listed on page 98 ($2,000,000 in 2006, 2007, and 2008). An A-B trust, established while you and your spouse are alive, essentially allows you to double the money you can leave to your beneficiaries without incurring estate taxes, depending on how you hold title to your assets and how much each of you owns.

What is the difference between an A-B trust and a revocable living trust?

Revocable living trusts are primarily meant to avoid probate fees, to transfer the legal titles to your assets as quickly as possible to beneficiaries, and to protect you if you become incapacitated. A-B trusts can save your beneficiaries significant estate taxes if you are married and expect to have an estate valued at more than the allowable non-taxable amounts.

How does an A-B trust work?

Let's say you have real estate and other income and assets worth about $4,000,000, owned equally by each of you. If you create an A-B trust, if you died, say, in 2006 your "half share" of the estate, in this case $2,000,000, will pass into either the A or B portion of the trust rather than directly to your spouse. (You will decide with your attorney if you will select the A or B portion.) For this example, we will determine that your portion will pass into the A part of the trust at your death. Your spouse can be the trustee of the trust and can receive any income it produces or, at the discretion of the trustee subject to an ascertainable standard, access the principal of the A trust for as much as is needed for his or her health, support, maintenance, and education. For the surviving spouse, all of this basically operates practically as if the money weren't in a trust.

But here is the difference: When the second spouse dies, both the A and B portions of the trust are passed on to the beneficiaries, but because the A portion went directly into an estate-tax-saving trust, it never became a part of the surviving spouse's estate. This means that the beneficiaries can receive the A part of the trust with your spouse's estate tax exemption applied to it and the B part of the trust with your estate tax exemption applied to it at your death. If the estate is valued at $4,000,000, that means that the beneficiaries will not owe any estate taxes, because they will technically be receiving $2,000,000 from each partner rather than $4,000,000 from one partner. If the first to die has assets above the exemption amount ($2,000,000 in the year 2006), then the excess needs to go to the surviving spouse, either outright or in the right kind of trust to defer taxes on the first death.

If you want to give your spouse the right to receive income from your assets during his or her lifetime but no say as to who inherits your portion of the trust after your spouse's death, you may also want to consider a variation on an A-B trust. This type of arrangement may involve a QTIP trust (explained later) as one of the trusts. If you and/or your spouse have children from previous relationships, this is something to think about.

That sounds great, but there is no way that my estate is going to be worth $4,000,000. So I don't have to think about an A-B trust, right?

Four million is not the magic number. If you and your spouse together have property valued above the exempt amount ($2,000,000 in the year 2006), an A-B trust may benefit you. If you own your home outright, for example, control any business interests, or have any interest in a retirement plan, pension, or other investments, you may be surprised at how quickly the value of your estate adds up. If you have owned your home for a long time, it is likely that its value has increased substantially and, given the performance of the stock market over time, the same may be true of investments you've held for many years. Make sure that you are counting everything you will leave behind, including your life insurance policy, any retirement plans with death benefits, art, and antiques, before you make any trusts decisions based on the value of your estate.

Is there a limit to the amount of assets a husband and wife together can shelter in an A-B trust?

Yes. Here are the maximum amounts for estate credits for current and future years:

FOR THOSE DYING IN	MAXIMUM ESTATE CREDIT IS
2006–2008	$4,000,000
2009	$7,000,000
2010	Unlimited

Are A-B trusts only for married couples?

Yes, if they involve the unlimited marital deduction. (Remember, married couples can leave each other as much as they want, and the surviving spouse will pay no estate tax.) But unmarried couples, same-sex couples, or any two people can set up A-B trusts that will remain in place until both partners have died. The tax benefits will be experienced by those who receive the assets after both partners have died. But there is no comparable tax deferral for unmarried couples like the unlimited marital deduction between spouses.

What is a bypass trust?

Also called a life-estate trust, a bypass trust lets unmarried partners each create a trust that, in the event of the first partner's death, pays income to the surviving partner for life. At the second death, the remaining assets in each trust go to their respective beneficiaries.

I am a widow. Is it too late for me to create an A-B trust?
I'm afraid so. Both spouses must be alive at the time you set up an A-B trust. However, if less than nine months have passed since your husband's death and you have not accepted the benefits of an asset, you may be able to arrange to "disclaim" your interest in part of his estate and achieve the same result. Without a formal disclaimer trust (a variation on an A-B trust that also must be set up before either spouse's death), however, your disclaimer will keep your husband's assets out of your estate but won't let you benefit from them. The assets will pass as if you were deceased. You must see a trust lawyer to disclaim your interest in your inheritance, but it may well be worth your while.

Who will really benefit from an A-B trust?
Your beneficiaries, who are usually your children, will enjoy the tax savings from this trust. With or without an A-B trust, a deceased husband or wife can pass assets to the other spouse with the unlimited marital deduction, which means without any estate tax at all at the first death, but a potentially gigantic estate tax at the second death.

What happens if both partners die at the same time? In that case, will an A-B trust still benefit the beneficiaries?
Yes, the trust should have a simultaneous death provision, which says that if it is impossible to establish the order of death, then for the sake of funding the A-B trust the less wealthy spouse survived the wealthier spouse. This helps protect the benefit.

How much will it cost to set up an A-B trust and have it funded?
Your A-B trust could cost between $2,000 and $3,000 to set up, depending on how many assets need to move into it. The

more real estate and other title transfers you have, the more it will cost you to establish the trust.

OTHER KINDS OF TRUSTS

SPECIAL-NEEDS TRUSTS

A special-needs trust is designed to permit funds to be held in trust for the benefit of a developmentally disabled person throughout his or her lifetime without making him or her ineligible to receive public benefits such as Supplemental Security Income (SSI) and Medicaid. The purpose of this type of trust is to supplement government aid without causing a loss of that aid. As a result, the terms of the trust need to be very restrictive.

The trustee of a special needs trust must be aware of the rules regarding distributions for SSI purposes. Currently, if you give an SSI recipient food, cash, clothing, or shelter paid for with funds from the trust, these gifts are supposed to be reported to the SSI representative. The following month's SSI check will be reduced by the value of the gift. For example, if I give a disabled person $100 from the trust, he will receive $100 less from SSI the next month. The trustee can, however, pay for dental work, utilities, phone bills, a car, car insurance, vacations, and basically anything else that does not come under the heading of food, money, clothes, or shelter—which SSI money is supposed to provide—without reducing the SSI recipient's monthly SSI income. It is difficult to find out the rules about such distributions, and they vary from state to state, but this should not stop you from creating such a trust for someone who truly needs it. It can be a great boon to the long-term care and happiness of your loved one.

I have two daughters, one of whom is disabled. Although I am concerned about the welfare of my child, a special needs trust seems very complicated. Couldn't I just leave everything to my healthy daughter, with the understanding that she will take care of her less fortunate sister?

I really discourage this, for the same reason that I discourage people from just gifting to their children to avoid probate fees. What if the daughter to whom you leave all your assets gets divorced and your ex-son-in-law makes a claim on half the money? What if your daughter gets into serious financial difficulty and a creditor or a court tries to attach her money? My point is that anything can happen, and your disabled daughter will not necessarily be protected.

Testamentary Trusts

A testamentary trust is a trust that is created via your will, after you have died. At that time, your assets are put in a testamentary trust by the order of a probate court judge.

Are testamentary trusts a good idea?

Since a testamentary trust is created through your will, it will have to go through probate. It's my belief that one should avoid probate wherever possible, so I don't recommend testamentary trusts.

Inter Vivos Trusts

Inter vivos trust is simply another name for a revocable living trust, which you establish while you are alive, as opposed to a testamentary trust, which is established in your will and doesn't become effective until after you die.

Totten Trusts

Totten trust is a term for a bank account that you set up with documentation stating you are the owner of the account and instructions that upon your death, the account is to be paid to your designated payee. If the payee is alive at the time of your death and an adult, he can receive the funds simply by producing your death certificate at the bank and proving his identity.

QPRT Trusts

A qualified personal residence trust (QPRT) is a kind of grantor-retained interest trust that can be used to pass a house out of an estate at a discounted value even if the trustor is still living in it. The purpose of this trust is to save on estate tax. Here's how it works: You choose a term of ownership of the house. At the end of this term, the house is distributed to someone you have designated in the trust agreement. (He or she may or may not let you live in it.) Once you put the house in the trust you can't take it back; it is considered a gift to the person, who will receive the house after your term of ownership is up. But since you retain an interest in the house for a number of years, the gift is not worth as much to the recipient as if you had given it to him outright. So, for example, you can pass a house worth $1,000,000 to your children for an estate-tax value of $500,000 if you put it in a QPRT with a 7.5-year term. As of 2007, if you are in the 45 percent estate-tax bracket, this could mean a savings of $225,000 in estate taxes. (If you die before the term expires, your children don't get the savings.) Once the house has been given to your children, if you continue to live in it you will need to pay them market-value rent (and if your child rents it to you and he or she dies, you may be dealing with a daughter- or son-in-law). The ability to move this money from your estate to your children as rent can be a further benefit of a QPRT trust. Note that with a QPRT your children's income tax basis may be lower than with an inheritance.

QTIP Marital Deductions

QTIP stands for qualified terminable interest property, and here's what it means: The spouse to die first can leave assets (above the estate-tax-exempt amount) in trust for the surviving spouse and have those excess assets taxed upon the death of the second spouse. The spouse who dies first may retain control of who inherits the estate upon the death of the spouse who dies second. So, effectively, there is no estate tax due on the first death. Among the requirements for this type of trust is that the surviving spouse must be entitled to all the income of the trust at least once per year. The surviving spouse may not assign this right to anyone else.

Charitable Remainder Trusts

There are different forms of this type of trust, but, basically, if a charitable remainder trust is established, it means that you have given your assets in trust to benefit a tax-qualified charity (which gives you an income-tax deduction) but that you can receive income based on the value of the assets you have given away for as long as you are alive. This type of trust is very good for people who have assets that have gone up in value significantly since they bought them. If they need income and don't want to lose dollars to capital-gains tax when they sell their assets, this trust allows the assets to be sold income-tax-free, so that every dollar is available to earn income for the beneficiary. However, at death, the entire principal of the trust is paid to the charity (and not to other beneficiaries, such as your children). In the year you set up such a trust, you will receive an income tax deduction, which can be spread out over five years. So, for example, if you make a gift of $100,000 in this way, you will receive tax benefits that will give you back as much as $50,000 of the gift. Every university and charity with a planned giving department can run the figures for you for free.

Does it make more sense to give money to charity or to let my children inherit it?

That depends on your financial situation and your desires. But if your children or other beneficiaries are going to be paying estate tax and income tax on what they inherit, it may make more sense to give some assets away and get a tax deduction now, or to leave some of your assets to charity upon your death. For instance, if you name a tax-exempt organization such as a church, school, or animal shelter as the beneficiary of any tax-deferred plans (for example, IRAs or Keoghs), the organization—unlike individual beneficiaries—will not have to pay income tax on the distribution. One hundred percent of the money will go to the charity because charitable organizations are not subject to estate tax. Let's say you are in the 55 percent estate-tax bracket and that your beneficiaries will have to pay 28 percent federal and 7 percent state tax on the proceeds of your retirement account. It is possible that as much as 90 percent of your IRA will go to the government! This would be a good time to think of the great work that private charitable organizations do. Private charities and social programs flourish in the United States because our tax laws encourage generous giving. See the upcoming section on gifting for more information on this option.

Life Insurance Trusts

I hope that by the time you die you will no longer have or need life insurance (please see *Ask Suze About... Insurance*), but if you do still have it, a life insurance trust is a type of trust that protects life insurance proceeds from estate taxes. A life insurance trust makes the trust, rather than you as an individual, the owner of the policy. Consult an attorney before you buy life insurance if you think you might want to do this, as it is best to create the trust before you buy the insurance.

Do I need a life insurance trust?

Young families frequently carry high amounts of term insurance in order to protect their children in the event of the premature death of a parent. Since the proceeds of these policies are included when calculating the value of an estate, a lot of that protection may be lost to estate taxes. If you take out $500,000 or more of coverage, you may want to discuss this option with a trust attorney.

Grantor-Retained Annuity Trusts

A grantor-retained annuity trust (GRAT) can be used to reduce taxes on your estate by sheltering shares of company stock. You can reserve the right to receive payments each year from the shares held within the trust for a designated period of time. When the period of time that you designate is over, those assets will be gifted to whomever you have chosen to receive them. The gift to your beneficiaries is based on the size of the gift less the amount of income you receive from the trust. In other words, if your stocks were worth $150,000 at the time of your gift and you received $35,000 in income from the trust, the gift will be valued at $115,000 (less than the $150,000 that would otherwise be taxable in your estate)—a pretty good savings.

A note of caution: Choose the length of time you wish to receive income from the trust carefully. If you die before the transfer goes into effect, the trust will dissolve and the stocks will be considered part of your estate.

Titling Assets

Titles to assets affect your will, living trust, estate tax, income tax, and possibly property tax.

Joint Tenancy with Right of Survivorship (JTWROS)

Joint tenancy with right of survivorship allows two or more people to hold the title to an asset. If one person dies, the title immediately transfers into the name of the other joint tenants without having to go through probate.

A potential problem with joint tenancy with right of survivorship, though, is that it will override any provisions in your will or living trust. There are many good reasons for you to hold something in joint tenancy, but trying to use it as a substitute for a will (or a trust) is not one of them.

Do all states have joint tenancy laws?
A few states—Alaska, North Carolina, Pennsylvania, South Carolina, Tennessee, and Texas, among them—have specific limitations about what can be held in joint tenancy, such as only real estate, or who can hold this type of title, such as only spouses. You should check with an attorney who specializes in estate planning and knows the laws of your state.

Is my house the only thing I can hold in joint tenancy?
No. Real estate is the most common thing held in joint tenancy, but bank accounts and other assets with titles can also be held this way.

What about holding a bank account in joint tenancy? How does that work?
Many people hold their checking or savings accounts, or their certificates of deposit, in JTWROS, which requires only that all the joint "tenants" sign as such when the account is opened. When one joint tenant dies, the surviving joint tenant (or tenants) may continue to use the account without having to go through probate, and automatically inherit the deceased tenant's share of the account.

My husband and I own everything in joint tenancy with right of survivorship (JTWROS) and I am the sole beneficiary of his life insurance policy and IRA. How will the estate be settled when he dies?
You have done a pretty good job of minimizing the paperwork and time that will be involved in settling your husband's estate, unless you are in a community-property state, in which case you might be missing the step up in cost basis for your real estate. Otherwise, once the appropriate institutions have received a certified copy of your husband's death certificate (and any other documentation they may require), everything will simply switch over into your name. But this simplicity may come with a big cost down the road—increased estate taxes for your children because you didn't utilize a death-tax-saving trust.

What if my husband and I hold our house as joint tenants with right of survivorship but then we both die at the same time?
This is one of the drawbacks of using joint tenancy as an alter-

native to a will—there is no provision for an alternate beneficiary. If you have no other will or trust providing for the disposition of your house, the house would pass as if you had died intestate, with one part going to each of your blood relatives, in an order established by your state.

I've heard that once I hold something in JTWROS, I can't get a reverse mortgage if I want it. Is that true?
It's possible. A reverse mortgage is a kind of loan available to senior citizens who need extra income and own their homes outright, in which the homeowner receives monthly payments during his or her lifetime. The loan is repaid, plus interest and finance charges, after the death of the homeowner, by the beneficiaries. Since the age of the applicant for a reverse mortgage is relevant, if someone under age 62 (your child, for example) is a joint tenant on your house, you might not be eligible for a reverse mortgage.

My sister is in serious credit card debt, and we own property in joint tenancy. Can her creditors come after my share of the property?
The general rule is that your sister's creditors can only come after her half of the property, but this is a tricky area of the law, so be careful.

My daughter and I hold the title to our house in JTWROS. Now she and her husband are getting a divorce, and I want to move to my daughter's state in order to be closer to her and my grandchildren during this difficult time. The problem is that my son-in-law's lawyer says that I will need my son-in-law's signature in order to sell my house, because he is still legally married to my daughter and therefore entitled to an interest in her half of my house! Can this be true?

Unfortunately, it is true. You will have to wait to sell your property until your son-in-law signs those papers or until his divorce from your daughter is finalized, even though his name is not on the title. Title companies do not like to take any chances. They will want to make sure her husband does not make a claim. A title company can require more of you than the law does. So, while a transfer of ownership may be legal, the title company can still refuse to insure the title to a new buyer if you don't meet their requirements.

My neighbor held her house in joint tenancy with her oldest son, with the understanding that when she died, he would sell it and share the proceeds with her other two sons. She thought this would be a good way to avoid probate fees. But then her oldest son died a month after she did, before he had changed his will or done anything with his mother's house. His wife has inherited the house, and now she is refusing to share anything with the two surviving sons, who will have to go to court to try to get the house back. Isn't this unfair?

Yes, it is. But even if your neighbor's oldest son had changed his will to leave that house to his two brothers, in some states his wife would have still been entitled to as much as half the house, if she decided to challenge the will. If only your neighbor had set up a trust or held a title in all three sons' names, this terrible situation could have been avoided.

It seems like a will doesn't matter if you hold your property in joint tenancy. Is that true?

I'm afraid it is. If you own property as a joint tenant and you die first, that property passes immediately to your joint owner, even if you leave a will that says it's to go to someone else. Assets held in joint tenancy are not subject to a will, and will always be awarded to the surviving joint tenant.

Once I hold property in joint tenancy, can I ever take it back and hold it separately again?

When you terminate joint tenancy, it turns into tenants-in-common or co-tenancy, in which each party owns his or her share of the property outright. You won't get the whole property back even if you were the one who put the name(s) on the title, unless the other tenant agrees to sign it over to you or let you buy his or her share.

How is the estate tax figured on a piece of jointly held property?

For joint tenants other than spouses, the estate tax will be based on the amount of money you invested when you created or bought the property. In other words, if you paid for the entire property when it was first purchased, then the full value of the property should be allocated to your estate for tax purposes.

If joint tenants are not married, the IRS assumes that the joint tenant who dies first is the one who made the entire investment. Unless you can offer proof that the surviving tenant did so as well, the property will be taxed 100 percent to the estate of the first to die. There are special rules for married couples, depending on when an asset was purchased.

If I make my son a joint tenant with right of survivorship in my home, can he then take control of at least some of my affairs if I become incapacitated?

Actually, this sort of joint tenancy is a potential problem, particularly if one of the parties becomes incapacitated. Everyone on a joint tenancy title of a house needs to be able to sign the necessary documents in order to do anything with the house. Say you were incapacitated and in need of long-term care, and your son decided he needed to sell or refinance your house in order to pay for your medical expenses. As a joint tenant, your son will still need your signature on any documents, which, since you are incapacitated, you may be unable to provide. Your son will have to go to court and have the court appoint a conservator for your interests, and the court will be the one signing off on your son's decisions.

In this situation you are better off setting up a trust and making your son a successor trustee. If you are incapacitated, this will let him act independently on legal matters without having to get court approval.

My wife and I hold our property in joint tenancy, but we are separating. I'm moving to another state, and my wife is going to stay in our house and keep up the payments until we sell it, when she'll receive a bigger share of the proceeds in exchange for taking care of it now. Does this seem like a reasonable plan?

I'm sorry to say that this plan leaves you extremely vulnerable. What happens if your wife fails to keep up with the mortgage payments or taxes on your house? What if something happens to your wife and she dies before the house is sold? Change the title to equal tenants-in-common right away.

My brother and his wife held their house in a joint tenancy, but after she died my brother was told that he had to file papers with his county clerk, who required a tax clearance from the probate court in order to file the forms! Wasn't avoiding probate the whole point of holding something in joint tenancy?

Some states or local governments require people who own property in joint tenancy to file papers with a local clerk in order to formally transfer ownership after one tenant dies. And some county clerks won't record the necessary forms without proof of a tax clearance—which, of course, sends you right back to a probate court. Again, if your state or local government requires this, you can avoid probate by holding that property in a revocable living trust. This is another reason to check the laws of your particular state before assigning title to assets.

Tenancy by the Entirety

About 30 states allow you and your spouse to hold real estate in tenancy by the entirety, which means that neither one of you can transfer the property while you are both alive without the other's permission. This is because each of you owns the entire property as opposed to an equal share of it. Only real estate can be held in this type of tenancy, and only legally married couples can have this type of tenancy.

Tenancy-in-Common (TIC)

When a property is held as tenants-in-common, it is owned by multiple individuals who each hold an undivided proportionate interest in the property. Each person can own a different percentage. Anything you own as a tenant-in-common will be subject to probate. Or you can transfer your shares in the property into a living trust and avoid probate.

My sisters and I are joint tenants with right of survivorship in a summer home. We all want our children to inherit our individual parts of the house after we die. We have designated that in our wills—will that accomplish what we want?
If you and your sisters own a house as joint tenants with right of survivorship, upon your death, your surviving sisters, not your children, will automatically inherit your portion of the home. If you and your sisters were to change how you hold title to tenants-in-common, on the other hand, you could leave

your share in the house to your children, but, remember, your share would have to go through probate unless it was also held in a living trust. It's best to put your share in a trust and ask your sisters to do the same. That way, everyone is protected.

Community Property

Nine states (Arizona, California, Idaho, Louisiana, Nevada, New Mexico, Texas, Washington, and Wisconsin) have community-property laws, which define a particular form of co-ownership for married couples. While the particular laws in each state are different, as a general rule, community-property states hold that the income and property acquired by a married couple should be divided equally in the event of a divorce unless both spouses agree in writing to an alternate arrangement. Thus, all marital property in such a state is owned by you and your spouse equally; this includes all property acquired during the course of the marriage other than by gift or inheritance. As long as residents of community-property states keep their gifts and/or inheritances in their own individual names (John Doe, a married man, as his separate property) or a separate trust, and do not commingle them by depositing them in joint accounts with their spouse, the gifts and/or inheritance will retain their separate property character.

Agreements changing the character of property from separate to community or vice versa must be in writing to be fully enforceable.

Please note: Five of the nine community-property states—Arizona, California, Nevada, Texas, and Wisconsin—let couples add the right of survivorship to community property, permitting you to bypass probate and transfer title automatically at death. The only drawback: If both partners die simultaneously, the property goes to probate.

Does this mean that in a community-property state I would have no claim to my husband's half of our property?

The answer is yes. Generally, you are entitled to half of anything acquired during your marriage while you were living in a community-property state, but your spouse has the right to dispose of his half of the property as he wishes.

If I live in a community-property state, what is the best way to take title of property?

It depends. The best way to take title for assets that go up in value after the date of purchase in a community-property state is in community property, not joint tenancy with right of survivorship.

I'll illustrate this with an example. Let's say that you and your spouse bought $10,000 worth of a certain stock many years ago and you have been holding it in joint tenancy. The IRS will consider that $10,000 to be the cost basis of the stock for tax purposes, which means that you will owe capital gains taxes on the profit you will make when you sell the stock, assuming it has gone up in price. By holding the stock in joint tenancy with your spouse, you are each entitled to half the cost basis—in this case, $5,000.

Now, we'll say that the stock is worth $100,000 when your spouse dies. Because you held the stock in joint tenancy, you will receive a step up in tax basis of your deceased spouse's half of the stock equal to fair market value at the time of his death. In this case, that half would increase to a tax basis of $50,000 while the tax basis of your half of the stock would remain at $5,000. Since you own the stock by yourself now, the new tax basis on that same $100,000 worth of stock is $55,000 ($50,000 plus $5,000). If you sold it today you would only have to pay capital-gains tax on $45,000, or the amount of your gain ($100,000 – $55,000).

Next, let's look at what would happen to this scenario if you lived in a community-property state and held the stocks in title as community property. Just as in joint tenancy, you each will have an original cost basis of $5,000. However, when your spouse dies, each half will receive a step up in tax basis—both your spouse's half and your own. Both halves will step up to $50,000, for a total tax basis of $100,000. Therefore, if you sold the stock for $100,000, you wouldn't have to pay any capital-gains tax at all. That's a huge savings! However, if the stock goes down in value, both halves with community property will get a step down in tax basis.

If I live in a community-property state, can I hold assets in joint tenancy with someone other than my spouse?

If the asset is separate property, sure. But if the asset is community property, then your spouse would have a claim against you and the other joint tenant for the interest he or she would be entitled to under community-property law.

What if I own property from the time before I got married?

The property itself will usually be considered separate, as long as you are careful not to mix your individual property with community property that you have acquired during your marriage. If you make income on that property during your marriage, however, the income may be considered community property. Because the laws are changing fast in this area, it really would be best to spell this out in a prenuptial agreement.

I live in a community-property state. Is my wife automatically entitled to half of my life insurance too, even if I name someone else as a beneficiary?

If you paid the insurance premiums with community-property dollars, then, yes, unless you and your spouse have an agreement to the contrary.

GIFTING

Gifting can be a great way to minimize the size of your estate and, subsequently, your estate taxes, but be careful, for there are more pitfalls in this part of the law than many people are aware of. Gifting and estate limits are closely intertwined. Read on.

How much money can I give away each year without having to file a gift-tax return?
You can give $12,000 each year (as of 2006) to as many individuals as you want without paying a gift tax and without filing a gift tax return. This limit is rising and will be indexed for inflation. However, the increase is very modest.

Can my husband and I each give away $12,000 per year to the same person, or must only one of us give?
You each can give $12,000 per year to as many people as you'd like, even if you have recipients in common.

My daughter really needs money. What would happen if I gave her more than $12,000 in one year?
You will need to file a gift-tax return. In the year 2006, for example, in addition to the $12,000 per year, per person gift exemption, you are also limited to a total of $1,000,000 in gifts over the course of your lifetime. What this means is that if you have not exceeded the annual per year, per person limit, there would be no gift or estate tax owed on the first $1,000,000 of your estate. Whatever amount over $12,000 you have given

away in any one year to the same person will be subtracted from this lifetime gift exemption.

In other words, you and your husband can each give your daughter $12,000 per year, for a total of $24,000 each year, without any tax consequences. If, in one year, each of you gave her, say, $25,000, you would each need to file a gift-tax return for $13,000, which is the amount by which your gift exceeds the annual limit. That $13,000 would be subtracted from your lifetime maximum gift figure. So if you and your husband died in 2006 and left everything outright to each other and wasted one of your tax exemptions, your heirs would owe taxes after the first $987,000 ($1,000,000 minus the $13,000 gift above the $12,000 annual exclusion).

Is the gift tax a federal or state tax?

There are two levels of taxation—federal and state. The federal tax is due to the IRS and is computed by looking at the total of all gifts made during your life and what you leave at death.

The state gift tax is paid to the state of residence and due only on gifts made during life. Connecticut, Louisiana, North Carolina, and Tennessee are the states that impose a state gift tax.

Can't I avoid all this hassle and just put my kids' names on my accounts as co-owners?

You could, and if everything goes smoothly, they will avoid probate but not necessarily gift or estate taxes. But this makes you vulnerable to other difficulties.

If your children are sued for any reason (say they cause a car accident or someone injures himself on their property) and there is a judgment against them, any assets you have put their name on could be used to pay that judgment. Similarly, if your children get into trouble with the IRS, your shared assets are now in danger, because they belong, at least on paper, to your child as well as to you.

Co-owning assets may also create unintended gift tax consequences for your children. If you add your children's names to the title of your house, for example, it may be construed by the IRS as a gift, since your children did not contribute to the purchase price of your home. Once you put them on the title, you can't take them off without their signatures. And once you record any document, it becomes a part of the public record, and you can't act as if it never happened.

What if I just give my children my assets?

Well, if your estate is not going to be worth more than the lifetime gift/estate maximum ($2,000,000 in 2006), then you don't really need to put things in your children's names for estate tax purposes, since there won't be any estate taxes to pay. If your estate is going to be worth more than this, you should consult a lawyer with some expertise in estate planning before you simply give any of your assets away. By making a gift, you may cost your children income tax by them losing the step up in cost basis inherited assets may receive.

My mom gave me her home and all her stocks before she went into a nursing home. She has since died. Do I now owe estate and income tax on what she left me?

The amount you owe for estate taxes depends on the unified credit exemption for the year in which your mother died. The unified credit exemption is the amount your beneficiaries can inherit from you without having to pay federal estate taxes. If your mom died in 2006, you will pay federal estate taxes up to 46 percent on every dollar over $2,000,000. If your mom died in 2007, you will pay federal estate taxes up to 45 percent on every dollar over $2,000,000.

Unified Credit Exemption

FOR DEATHS OCCURRING IN	HIGHEST ESTATE EXEMPTION	HIGHEST ESTATE & GIFT-TAX RATE
2006	$2,000,000	46%
2007	$2,000,000	45%
2008	$2,000,000	45%
2009	$3,500,000	45%

Income tax works differently. Stocks and real estate that you inherit will not be taxed until you sell them, and the amount of tax you will owe will depend on your tax basis (see the answer to the next question). Also, if your mom received any type of Medicaid assistance prior to her death, the state may attempt to recover the costs of such assistance through these assets.

What difference does it make whether my mom gave me her stock while she was alive or if I inherited it after her death?

Actually, it makes a big difference. If your mom left you her assets after she died, you'd have inherited them. When you inherit something, you get a step up (or down) in tax basis on that asset. That means that if your mom bought stock in a company for $10,000 20 years ago, $10,000 is the cost basis—the original price—for that stock. If she left the stock to you in her will or revocable living trust, your tax basis will be the value of the stock at the time she died. This gives you a terrific benefit. If that stock was worth $200,000 at her death, then your tax basis for tax purposes is going to be $200,000. When you go to sell the stock, you will only owe capital-gains tax on anything worth more than $200,000. Your cost basis went from $10,000 to $200,000.

Now, if your mom gave you the same stock while she was

still alive, you'd have received it as a gift. Along with the title to that gift, you also receive your mom's original cost basis on the asset, which was $10,000. You're not entitled to a step up in tax basis with a gift. So if you sell the stock, now worth $200,000, you will owe taxes on $190,000. You will pay 15 percent of $190,000 to Uncle Sam, plus whatever your state charges for capital gains. Therefore, if your mom has assets such as stock or real estate that have increased in value since she bought them, her beneficiaries will save a great deal of income tax if they receive these assets after she dies.

I own my own business. Is it a good idea to give my children stock in my business before I die?

If your business is doing well and the value of that stock is increasing steadily, then giving away some of your stock now will allow them to keep its appreciated value since it's been transferred out of your estate. But remember, if their names are on the stock and if you want to sell the company later in life, you will need your children's agreement. (And they may leave stock to a spouse or others if they die before you.) Again, the stock is also subject to capital-gains tax, and your children will not receive a step up in cost basis as they would have if they'd inherited the stock after your death.

What if my parents make me a joint tenant but just don't file the paperwork? Can we avoid these taxes that way?

Many people do this, either because they think they can avoid taxes or they don't know that they need to file paperwork beyond adding a new name to the title of their property. But when your parents die, you will need to file an estate tax return for them if the value of the assets is above the exempt amount, and on the return is a section that will ask you to list all the property that your parents held in joint tenancy. You will want to answer this honestly, because the IRS can ask you to prove that you either purchased the property or filed a gift tax return for the gift. If your parents did not file a gift tax return, you could be subject to penalties on top of the gift tax. The maximum penalty for failure to report is the tax you owe plus a 75 percent penalty and interest calculated from the date that the tax would have been due.

My parents have given me their home as an outright gift (although they still live there) because it seemed to make sense to them at the time. What steps should I now take to make sure that if I were to die before them, they wouldn't have to go through probate and pay taxes on their house?

The best way to protect anything they have already given to you is to put it all in a revocable living trust and designate whether the property should go outright or in trust to your parents, if they are still alive at the time of your death.

Is there ever any circumstance in which my mother could give me something in joint tenancy and we would not owe gift taxes?

There are a few such cases, for example, if your mom buys U.S. savings bonds in joint tenancy or if she creates a joint convenience bank account (to which she contributes all the money).

Are the gifts I leave to a charity upon my death subject to estate tax?

No. Gifts to charity are free from taxation and are not considered a part of an estate for estate tax purposes.

Can I give as much money to charity as I want?

In many states there are limitations on how much you can give to a charity if you have a surviving spouse or children. If you are not married and are childless, then there are no limits to what you can donate.

At what point does gifting to a charity become a true estate-planning tool for me to consider?

If you are a married couple and have an A-B trust in the year 2006 with combined assets exceeding $4,000,000, or you are an individual with an estate that will be worth more than $2,000,000, you may want to consider charitable gifting. Your decision depends on your age, whether you have long-term health-care insurance, the financial situation of your children, and many other factors. Be sure to consult an attorney if you are in this category, as your state's tax rules for gifting also must be considered. Discuss your goals for gifting fully before making a decision. Ask yourself (and your financial adviser) the following questions:

- What is the purpose of my gift?
- Does it make sense in the context of my personal situation?
- If gifting seems appropriate, which assets should be gifted?

POWER OF ATTORNEY

A power of attorney is a document that authorizes another person to act for you as if they were you. This person is called your "agent" or your "attorney-in-fact." You can have a very broad power of attorney, which allows someone else to do things that usually only you can do, such as write checks from your bank accounts, pay your bills, or sign documents on your behalf. Alternatively, you can have a very limited power of attorney, which may authorize someone to do just one particular thing for you.

In my opinion, the best power of attorney is one that is authorized by a specific state law (also known as a statutory power of attorney); is a general power of attorney; and survives the incapacity of the maker. These three factors will give you the greatest ease in getting people and institutions to cooperate with you when you transact business through a power of attorney. However, a general power of attorney has been called a license to steal, since it's like a blank check.

Bear in mind that certain institutions may refuse to honor your power of attorney if it is not in the form the institution itself prints, even if it is a statutory form. The IRS requires you to use only their form for power of attorney, for example. Also, if you try to limit the scope of the power of attorney or make it too specific, brokerage houses may not want to accept it because they feel it does not cover all the types of actions they deem necessary. Finally, your power of attorney needs to be "durable"—to remain in effect if you become incapacitated—as this is the main reason for any power of attorney.

What is the difference between a power of attorney and a durable power of attorney?

A power of attorney authorizes someone to make legal and financial decisions on your behalf while you are alive. But, generally, if you become incapacitated, the power of attorney becomes void. A durable power of attorney stays in effect even after you are incapacitated, which is when you really need someone you trust making decisions for you. Keep in mind, though, that all powers of attorney die with the maker. So once the person who gave you the authority dies, you no longer can legally sign for anything as the person's agent. Such an act constitutes an ethical breach that could be used against you if there were any future disputes with heirs or creditors or the IRS.

What is the difference between a durable power of attorney for financial matters and a durable power of attorney for health care?

A durable power of attorney for financial matters deals only with financial matters. The durable power of attorney for health care (also called, depending on your state, a medical power of attorney, health-care proxy, or medical proxy) is a document you create to give your agent the authority to make health-care decisions for you as if he or she were you. This may include the authority to take you off life support.

If you don't give someone this power, it will be almost impossible for your loved ones to take you off life support, if it comes to that, even if they know that this is what you would have wanted. Remember, you have a right to die, but you cannot exercise that right unless you put your wishes in writing.

What is an agent?

This is the person empowered to make decisions for you under the durable power of attorney.

I already have a living will. Do I still need the durable power of attorney for health care?

Yes, because the two documents have different purposes. The durable power of attorney for health care lets you designate a person who can take you off life support (and to dictate under what circumstances) and to make less drastic medical decisions, too. A living will gives guidance to a doctor as to what types of medications you would want, but it does not authorize anyone to make decisions for you. Also, living wills cannot be changed significantly if your needs should change. I strongly recommend a durable power of attorney for health care as the most efficient and effective way to deal with your medical needs should you become incapacitated.

Some lawyers don't use anything but the power of attorney for health care since only this document gives someone other than your doctor decision-making power. The durable power of attorney for health care shifts the decision-making power from the doctor to your agent as soon as your doctor determines that you are no longer able to make decisions for yourself. This happens when you are unconscious or delirious, for example. You can tell your agent your preferences for treatment, but if there are unexpected circumstances, the agent will not be locked into what was written in a directive years before. The one thing I advise you to write out is that the management of pain is of primary importance to you.

If there aren't any circumstances under which I would want to be taken off life support, then I don't need to bother with the durable power of attorney, right?

Quite the contrary. You can state in your durable power of attorney for health care that you want heroic measures taken to save your life, no matter what kind of prognosis you might have for recovery. That is the point of the durable health power of attorney—that there will be a document that lets your family and your doctors know definitively what your wishes are if and when you can't communicate them.

Here are the three basic options that people generally choose from:

1. You want to prolong your life as long as possible, without regard to your condition, chance of recovery, or the cost of treatment.

2. You want life-sustaining treatment to be provided unless you are in a coma or ongoing vegetative state, which two doctors, one of whom is your attending physician, will determine in their best judgment.
3. You do not want your life to be unnaturally prolonged, unless there is some hope that both your physical and mental health might be restored.

Now, please keep in mind that this is an emerging area of the law. The U.S. Supreme Court granted the right to die less than 15 years ago. This landmark case said that if you have expressed your wishes in writing about the manner of your death in a clear and convincing fashion, doctors must honor it. Each state has come up with its own definition of what qualifies as "clear and convincing." This does not mean that every doctor will abide by them. A recent study indicated that in as many as 50 percent of cases, doctors do not follow the known wishes of the person. One reason may be that the doctors did not know about the existence of the patient's document. So be sure to send copies to your physicians and ask them to make the copies a permanent part of your medical records. Be sure your relatives have copies, too.

Most major hospitals now have ethics committees to help with difficult situations, so if you feel a situation merits some intervention, ask if you can speak to someone from the hospital ethics committee.

Should I choose the same person to be my attorney-in-fact for my durable power of attorney and my durable power of attorney for health care?

That is entirely up to you. Remember that, particularly in terms of your durable power of attorney for health care, whoever you select as your agent must be strong enough to act in accordance with your wishes, even if your loved ones strongly disagree. You should choose someone in whom you have confidence, who lives no more than a day's travel away, and with whom you have discussed your preferences for health care. Also consider whether your agent has too much of a conflict of interest (if, say, the person who can authorize pulling the plug also inherits a lot of money from you). If they have any hesitation about acting in that role, you should appoint someone else. If possible, it's also good to choose several alternate agents as well.

Can I make both of my daughters co-agents on my durable power of attorney for health care?

You can, if your state allows it, but I don't generally recommend it. Here's why: Even if you are very specific about your wishes, your agents will most likely have a lot of discretion to determine whether your medical circumstances meet the qualifications for carrying out your instructions. If your co-agents were to disagree with each other about anything, it is likely that no action would be taken, thus making all your planning worthless. In most cases, your child will consult with his or her siblings anyway, and you can express ahead of time your preference that he or she do so.

Another possibility is to make your other children backup agents. That means that you would have a second or third alternate agent if your first agent were unavailable for some reason.

A friend of mine had a durable power of attorney and appointed her daughter as her agent. But when the worst happened, her son went to court to try to stop her daughter from carrying out her wishes, saying that his mother had been incompetent when she signed the papers. Is there any way that situation could have been avoided?

Maybe not, but I would suggest doing two things. First, you want to talk to your family about your wishes beforehand so that they understand and respect them. Don't let anyone tell you this is too difficult or grim to talk about, because it is too important a matter not to discuss. If, after talking with your family, you get the feeling that certain family members might have difficulty carrying out your wishes, have the following sentence inserted into your durable power of attorney for health care: "I want the wishes of my agent to be respected regardless of the contrary wishes or intentions of other members of my family."

My mother had a durable power of attorney drawn up and made her brother attorney-in-fact. She is now in a nursing home, and my uncle is spending all her money on himself. What can we do?

This is why you really need to trust the person you name as your attorney-in-fact. You need to be sure that he or she will act in accordance with your wishes, in the best interests of you and the people who will be affected by your incapacity. While you can have a power of attorney revoked, it can take time and cost money. It depends on the state you live in, among other factors.

In some states, all that needs to happen is for the person who created the durable power of attorney to declare, preferably in the presence of witnesses, that he or she no longer wants the attorney-in-fact to keep acting in that capacity. The problem is that if the attorney-in-fact refuses to stop acting and still has copies of the original durable power of attorney, it may be difficult to prevent him or her from continuing to draw money out of accounts. How would banks know that the durable power of attorney has been revoked? You will probably need to see an attorney specializing in probate and trust litigation or elder-law litigation to resolve such a situation.

If your durable power of attorney has been recorded—that is, if it was taken to a county recorder's office and entered—you'll need to record a revocation, too.

This situation is yet another good example of why I believe so strongly in trusts. If you do have a rebel agent, it can be very tough to bring him or her in line: It may take a civil lawsuit, and that's expensive. If a trustee needs to be called to task, you usually have faster access to the probate court—a much better way to deal with the problem. If you are incapacitated, you can still be protected by the remainder beneficiaries of your trust, and, if the assets are moved, it will be easier to find them since they are in the name of the trust and not an individual agent.

Can I have a durable power of attorney in which the attorneys-in-fact are two people who must act jointly before they can do anything?

Yes, and although this will offer some protection in terms of making sure that one person doesn't violate your wishes, it can also slow things down. If you need a decision made immediately, requiring two people to sign off on everything might complicate matters.

Is it difficult to get a durable power of attorney for health care?

Not at all. Most states have a standard form for this, and many hospitals and public health services can provide it to you at no cost. You may want to speak with an attorney to help you fill it out, particularly if you have a special situation or particular illness that you want the form to cover. Choice in Dying has an excellent website, *www.choices.org*, from which you can download the relevant forms for your state.

How much should a durable power of attorney for health care cost me?

If an attorney is setting up a trust for you, the preparation for a durable power of attorney for health care should be included in his fee. In any case, it shouldn't cost more than $75 to $150.

Where should I store my durable power of attorney for health care?

You should always keep the original. Give a copy of the form to the person you have chosen to act as your agent, and send copies to your doctor and your health insurance company, to be kept as part of your medical records. This can be helpful if something happens while you are away from home, particularly if you keep the name of your doctor or insurance company in your wallet.

Once I draw up my durable power of attorney for health care, is it good forever?

Yes, although make sure to amend it if you experience a major change in your relationship, or if the person whom you have appointed as your agent dies. You can, of course, always change your durable power of attorney for health care if you change your mind about what kind of medical treatment you would want in dire circumstances.

I have a durable power of attorney for my mom, but the bank refuses to honor it. Does this happen often?

Because powers of attorney are so easily abused, many banks tend to be wary about accepting them. If your durable power of attorney is legitimate, a lawyer can help you get the bank to accept it, but this may take some time. If you have an incapacity clause in your revocable living trust, this situation can be avoided.

This is such a big problem that California created a statutory form for general power of attorney and passed a law that says if an institution refuses to honor the power of attorney in the statutory form, you can sue the institution and recover the costs of your suit, attorney fees, and damages. When they pass a law like that, you know it's been a problem!

If I live in a different state than my parents, and they want me to be their attorney-in-fact, do we need to set up the durable power of attorney in their home state?
The rules governing powers of attorney vary from state to state. I would recommend that you have the durable power of attorney drawn up by an attorney in the state in which your parents live.

What is a "springing" power of attorney?
This type of power of attorney, which is not legal in all states, becomes activated only when the person who draws it up becomes incapacitated. I don't recommend it—first, because it isn't accepted in all states, and, more important, because it isn't always clear what constitutes incapacity. Durable power of attorney is a much better choice.

Why don't more people have a durable power of attorney for health care?
I think it's simply because so many of us are afraid to confront our own mortality. Signing a paper like this makes death seem like an imminent reality, and that can provoke frightening and painful feelings. Another reason people don't sign such a power of attorney is they think they are too young to contemplate such things. But I promise you, no matter what your age, this is one of the most important things you can do to protect yourself and your finances.

Additional Resources

Durable Powers of Attorney for Health Care

National Hospice and Palliative Care Organization
1700 Diagonal Raod, Suite 625
Alexandria, VA 22314
(800) 658-8898
(703) 837-1500
www.caringinfo.org

General Information

The U.S. Administration on Aging
Washington, DC 20201
(202) 619-0724
www.aoa.gov

To find an attorney with experience in trusts and estates, contact:

The American College of Trust and Estate Counsel
3415 South Sepulveda Boulevard, Suite 330
Los Angeles, CA 90034
(310) 398-1888
(310) 572-7280 (fax)
www.actec.org

Consult the Martindale-Hubbell Law Directory, a nationwide listing of lawyers, at your local library or on the Internet at *www.martindale.com.*

Findlaw: Lawyer Search
www.lawyers.findlaw.com

American Academy of Estate Planning Attorneys
6050 Santo Road, Suite 240
San Diego, CA 92124
(800) 846-1555
www.aaepa.com

Nolo
950 Parker Street
Berkeley, CA 94710
(800) 728-3555
www.nolo.com
Easy-to-understand information available in the plain-English Law Center.

AARP
601 E Street NW
Washington, DC 20049
(888) 687-2277
www.aarp.org/estate_planning

Books

Gifting to People You Love: The Complete Family Guide to Making Gifts, Bequests, and Investments for Children by Adriane G. Berg. An essential guide to financial gift-giving, which includes basic information on small and large gifts, college savings, trusts, bequests, and investments.

Make Your Own Living Trust by Denis Clifford. This book explains how to create a living trust, transfer property to the trust, and amend or revoke the trust at any time.

Plan Your Estate by Denis Clifford and Cora Jordan. This informative book covers everything from the basics of wills and living trusts to sophisticated tax-saving strategies.

The American Way of Death Revisited by Jessica Mitford. This book is an exposé of the funeral industry.

8 Ways to Avoid Probate by Mary Randolph. This book details how to take advantage of eight important—and often overlooked—probate-avoidance strategies: set up payable-on-death bank accounts; name a beneficiary for retirement accounts; register stocks and bonds, and vehicles, in transfer-on-death forms; hold property in joint ownership; take advantage of special procedures for small estates; create a living trust; and give away property now.

Understanding Living Trusts: How You Can Avoid Probate, Save Taxes and Enjoy Peace of Mind by Vickie Schumacher. This book is an excellent guide that details living trusts.

Index

INDEX

About Suze Orman

Suze Orman has been called "a force in the world of personal finance" and a "one-woman financial advice powerhouse" by *USA Today*. A two-time Emmy® Award–winning television show host, *New York Times* best-selling author, magazine and online columnist, writer-producer, and motivational speaker, Suze is undeniably America's most recognized personal finance expert.

Suze has written five consecutive *New York Times* best sellers—*The Money Book for the Young, Fabulous & Broke*; *The Laws of Money, The Lessons of Life*; *The Road to Wealth*; *The Courage to Be Rich*; and *The 9 Steps to Financial Freedom*—as well as the national best sellers *Suze Orman's Financial Guidebook* and *You've Earned It, Don't Lose It*. Her most recent book, *Women & Money*, was published by Spiegel & Grau in February 2007. A newspaper column, also called "Women & Money," syndicated by Universal Press Syndicate, began in January 2007. Additionally, she has created *Suze Orman's FICO Kit, Suze*

Orman's Will & Trust Kit, *Suze Orman's Insurance Kit*, *The Ask Suze Library System*, and *Suze Orman's Ultimate Protection Portfolio*.

Suze has written, coproduced, and hosted five PBS specials based on her *New York Times* best-selling books. She is the single most successful fund-raiser in the history of public television, and recently won her second Daytime Emmy® Award in the category of Outstanding Service Show Host. Suze won her first Emmy® in 2004, in the same category.

Suze is contributing editor to *O, The Oprah Magazine* and *O at Home* and has a biweekly column, "Money Matters," on Yahoo! Finance. Suze hosts her own award-winning national CNBC-TV show, *The Suze Orman Show*, which airs every Saturday night, as well as *Financial Freedom Hour* on QVC television.

Suze has been honored with three American Women in Radio and Television (AWRT) Gracie Allen Awards. This award recognizes the nation's best radio, television, and cable programming for, by, and about women. In 2003, Suze garnered her first Gracie for *The Suze Orman Show* in the National/Network/Syndication Talk Show category. She won her second and third Gracies in the Individual Achievement: Program Host category in 2005 and 2006.

Profiled in *Worth* magazine's 100th issue as among those "who have revolutionized the way America thinks about money," Suze also was named one of *Smart Money* magazine's top thirty "Power Brokers," defined as those who have most influenced the mutual fund industry and affected our money, in 1999. A 2003 inductee into the Books for a Better Life (BBL) Award Hall of Fame in recognition of her ongoing contributions to self-improvement, Suze previously received the 1999 BBL Motivational Book Award for *The Courage to Be Rich*. As a tribute to her continuing involvement, in 2002 the organization established the Suze Orman First Book Award to honor a first-time author of a self-improvement book in any category. She received a 2003 Crossing Borders Award from the Feminist Press. The award recognizes a distinguished group of women who not only have excelled in remarkable careers but also have shown great courage, vision, and conviction by forging new places for women in their respective fields. In 2002, Suze was selected as one of five distinguished recipients of the prestigious TJFR Group News Luminaries Award, which honors lifetime achievement in business journalism.

A sought-after motivational speaker, Suze has lectured widely throughout the United States, South Africa, and Asia to audiences of up to fifty thousand people, often appearing alongside individuals such as Colin Powell, Rudy Giuliani, Jerry Lewis, Steve Forbes, and Donald Trump. She has been featured in almost every major publication in the United States and has appeared numerous times on *The View*, *Larry King Live*, and *The Oprah Winfrey Show*.

A Certified Financial Planner®, Suze directed the Suze Orman Financial Group from 1987 to 1997, served as vice president of investments for Prudential Bache Securities from 1983 to 1987, and from 1980 to 1983 was an account executive at Merrill Lynch. Prior to that, she worked as a waitress at the Buttercup Bakery in Berkeley, California, from 1973 to 1980.